RULERS OF INDIA-
RANJIT SINGH

RULERS OF INDIA-RANJIT SINGH

EDITOR

WILLIAM WILSON HUNTER

GYAN

Published by

GYAN

Gyan Publishing House
5, Ansari Road
Daryaganj, New Delhi-110002
Phone: 011-47034999, 9811692060
E-mail: books@gyanbooks.com

Distribution Network
gyanbooks.com
India, USA, Canada, UK, Australia

ISBN: 978-93-7133-057-2 (HB)

First Published, 1905

2nd Impression 2025

Printed at: Gyan Press, Delhi.

RULERS OF INDIA-RANJIT SINGH
Editor: WILLIAM WILSON HUNTER

Rulers of India

EDITED BY

SIR WILLIAM WILSON HUNTER, K.C.S.I., C.I.E.

M.A. (Oxford); LL.D. (Cambridge)

RANJÍT SINGH

CONTENTS

NOTE

The orthography of proper names follows the system adopted by the Indian Government for the *Imperial Gazetteer of India*. That system, while adhering to the popular spelling of very well-known places, such as Punjab, Poona, Deccan, etc., employs in all other cases the vowels with the following uniform sounds :—

a, as in woman : *á*, as in father : *i*, as in kin : *í*, as in intrigue : *o*, as in cold : *u*, as in bull : *ú*, as in rule.

Note to p. 25.

The administrative divisions have lately been enlarged and include more districts: but it is convenient to maintain the arrangement which prevailed during the twenty years subsequent to annexation.

Addition to Note, p. 138.

They had however been obviously utilized by Major Carmichael Smyth in his account of the reigning family of Lahore, although without any acknowledgment. This may have been due to prudential regard for Colonel Gardner's safety and position.

RANJÍT SINGH

CHAPTER I

INTRODUCTORY

THERE is, perhaps, no more notable and picturesque figure among the chiefs who rose to power on the ruins of the Mughal Empire than Mahárájá Ranjít Singh, the founder of the short-lived Sikh kingdom of Lahore. In the stormy days at the beginning of the century, amid a fierce conflict of races and creeds, he found his opportunity, and seizing it with energy, promptitude, and genius, he welded the turbulent and warlike sectaries who followed the teaching of Govind Singh into a homogeneous nation. Under his strong and remorseless rule, the Sikhs, trained and disciplined on a military system more perfect than had before or than has been since employed in the native States of India, were rapidly converted into a formidable fighting machine, which only broke in pieces when the folly and weakness of the great Mahárájá's successors persuaded them to use it against the English.

The Sikh monarchy was Napoleonic in the suddenness of its rise, the brilliancy of its success, and the completeness of its overthrow. Like his contemporary,

Napoleon Bonaparte, the Mahárájá of Lahore failed to found a lasting dynasty on the ruins of the petty States, Rájput, Muhammadan, and Sikh, which he in turn attacked and destroyed. His victories had no permanent result; his possessions, like a faggot of sticks, bound together during his lifetime by the force of his imperious will, fell asunder the moment the restraining band was severed. His throne and the tradition of his power and greatness passed into the hands of incompetent successors, who allowed the ship of the State to drift on to the rocks in irremediable wreck. It is very easy to stretch historical parallels too far, but the likeness between the character and fortunes of Napoleon and Ranjít Singh is not only striking in its superficial resemblance, but interesting as showing how similar conditions work out the same results in Asia as in Europe; among Frenchmen intoxicated with the first triumphant revolt against feudal tyranny, and Sikhs fresh from a revolt as momentous against the crushing spiritual despotism of Bráhmanism. The revolutionaries of the West and the East found their masters in Napoleon and Ranjít Singh, men of military genius, absolutely selfish, pitiless and immoral; but the power they seized they were unable to transmit to others. It is true that Napoleonism had in our day a late revival, but it did no more than emphasize the fact that adventurers do not easily found dynasties. The popular obedience is willingly given to the great captain, the leader of men, who seems in the dazzled eyes of the people to embody the spirit and glory of the country. But the glamour is personal to the man and does not transfigure his heirs and successors. Then, the throne founded by genius is seen to be a poor, tawdry thing, on the steps of which stand a crowd of greedy, unscrupulous parasites, who have no thought but of enriching themselves at the expense of the people. Discipline and obedience give place to conspiracy and revolt; enthusiasm is succeeded by contempt; till, ere long, the mushroom dynasty is extinguished amidst the laughter of those who applauded its birth. As it was with Napoleon and the Second Empire, so was it with Ranjít Singh and his son Kharak Singh and the bastards who quarrelled over the inheritance of the Lion of the Punjab.

Far different is the fate of august and ancient dynasties whose hereditary dignities have descended in an unbroken line through many generations. These fall, it is true, by the vices and recklessness of their representatives, as history has often shown. But how many chances are in their favour, and how criminal is the weakness and how abject the folly which alienate the easily retained affection of a nation! Whatever may be said of the divine right of kings, it would seem that the stars in their courses fight on their behalf; that something of divinity hedges them about; they are the object of a respect and love which is worth more to them than armies in battle array; the immemorial sentiment of mankind demanding a master, the weakness of humanity asking to be ruled, are the very foundations of their throne. A single mistake or a pungent epigram may cost the heir of an adventurer his crown; but the hereditary ruler can securely sit, like the Olympian gods, above the thunder. His mistakes are speedily forgotten, his follies are forgiven unto seventy times seven, and, if he falls, it is less from the waywardness of fortune than from his own determination to commit political suicide.

If this be the case in Europe, far more is it so in India, whose conservatism is intense, and where prescription and tradition and heredity outweigh, in popular estimation, any personal virtues of a ruler. In a country in which robbery and murder were honoured as hereditary occupations, and where dancing girls place their fragile virtue under the special protection of a deity, it will readily be understood that the splendid attributes of kingship gather around them a reverence and authority which are all but impregnable. Indian history, filled as it is with royal catastrophes and assassination and changing dynasties, does not, if read aright, conflict with the popular belief in the divine right of kings even to rule badly. India has had stormy experiences, and its rich provinces have been for many hundred years the coveted prize of successive hordes of invaders from the North-West, who have swept over the continent leaving ruin behind them, while the many hostile races and nations which make up its population have always been engaged in internecine strife. But the heart of the people of any particular State has almost invariably remained loyal to the hereditary local dynasty, and in good and evil fortune they have been willing to sacrifice themselves in its defence. Those principalities which have been strong enough to resist attack like Udaipur, Jaipur, and Jodhpur, or which have been happily placed far from the path of invaders, or hidden in the distant recesses of the Himalayas, such as Chamba, Mandi, and Suket, have existed under the rule of families so ancient that their genealogies are lost in prehistoric mist, and they proudly claim their ancestry in the Sun. Princes good and bad, beneficent and tyrannical, have ruled these States; but the people have accepted them, one and all, without a thought of revolt or resistance; and these same families will probably be still securely reigning over their ancient principalities when the conquest of India by England will be taught as ancient history in the Board Schools of a distant future. Many of these chiefships are as poor and weak as they are obscure and insignificant; a ruined castle, a few square miles of mountain and valley, a few hundred rupees of revenue, and an army the soldiers of which may be counted on the fingers of one hand. It is not material force which has given them a perennial stream of vitality. They have struck their roots deep, as trees grow in the rain and the soft air; they have, as it were, become one with nature, a part of the divine and established order of things; and the simple Rájput peasant no more questions their right to rule than he rebels against the sunshine which ripens his harvest or the storm which blasts it.

There are many principalities to-day in India, some of them of the first rank, whose history would seem, on superficial examination, to refute the idea that for the military adventurer the path of success is a difficult one. The great State of Haidarábád was founded by a rebellious viceroy of the Delhi emperors; the Maráthá States of Baroda, Gwalior, and Indore, and the Muhammadan chiefship of Bhopál were formed, in the last century, by successful generals of obscure origin; and the Mahárájás of Kashmír were created by the British Government in 1846. But it is most improbable that the ruling families in these States would have retained the power which was seized by their founders, had it not been for the circumstance that a strange and unknown volcanic force made its way through the soft and yielding strata of Indian society and crystallised them into their present form. This force was the rising power of the English, which, through the eighteenth and nineteenth centuries, ever increased in intensity. The victories of the British Government were won by gallantry or diplomacy, by force or by fraud; but its advance, though sometimes checked, was never long delayed. All the warlike races in India threw themselves by turns on this new and terrible enemy and were shattered and repulsed; till, at last, it stood revealed as the sole inheritor of the Empire of the Mughals and commanded peace throughout the continent, a peace which, with the single exception of the Mutiny, has remained unbroken for forty-five years. The Rájás and Nawábs who happened to be in possession when the English enforced their supremacy were confirmed in their rights.

Beati possidentes. Whatever may have been the method of acquisition, it was not for the English to question the divine right of conquest, or to deny that the sword was a valid title to inheritance. Thus it has happened that the Native Feudatory States of the present day can be roughly divided into two widely different classes, the first, respectable by antiquity and strong in the traditional loyalty of the people, the second, newer than the English Government itself and their origin the same—the violent disintegration of the Muhammadan Empire. Should the day ever come, as come it may, for time and change wait for all, when the English, weary of the burthen of rule, retire from India, the old Hindu principalities will survive the ensuing storm, as the mud-built villages with their mango groves are seen in times of flood high above the inundated country. But the new families whose birth was in war and plunder, who are alien in blood and race and creed to the people over whom they too often oppressively rule, and whose roots are not deep in the soil, will have to take their chance and fight again for their lands, as did the Sindhias and Holkars and Gáikwárs from whom they claim.

The downfall of the Sikh monarchy was chiefly due to the fact that the authority of Ranjít Singh was personal and drew no part of its strength from the inherent respect of the people for an ancient house. Sprung from the people and the outcome of the democratic principles of Sikhism, the one chance of the survival of his dynasty was that his successors should have inherited his character and ability. But this was not the case. His only son Kharak Singh was a hopeless imbecile; his grandson, Nao Nihál Singh, a youth of promise, died a violent death, and a period of anarchy set in which the men who succeeded had no power to subdue or control. There were several who claimed the throne as sons of the great Mahárájá, but the secrets of Ranjít Singh's zenána were the common property of the Lahore bazaars, and there was not one whose legitimacy the Sikhs accepted as proved. Then came the war with the English, in which the Sikhs, badly led, displayed the utmost gallantry in vain; ending in the occupation of the Punjab by a foreign army, dismemberment, and finally annexation. As Ranjít Singh had often prophesied, the red line marking the limit of British possessions moved on from the Sutlej to the Beas, thence to the Indus and the Afghán mountains, and all that remained to remind the world of the monarchy were an exiled prince at the Court of St. James and the ill-omened Koh-i-Núr in the regalia of the British Queen.

No man can be more strong than destiny. Although the hands of the English were clean in the matter of the Sikh wars and in the annexation of the Punjab, which were forced unwillingly upon them by the fierce and uncontrolled passions of the Sikh chiefs and people, yet there can be little doubt that, even if the contest with the English had been delayed, and the successors of Ranjít Singh had clung, as he did, to the British alliance, the trial of strength which was to determine the question of supremacy in Northern India must have occurred sooner or later. There were too many occasions for dispute and discord on the Sutlej and in Afghánistán; the temper of the Sikhs was so hot and imperious; the prestige of England was so essential to maintain, that it was impossible that these two military powers could have for long existed side by side in peace. It was fortunate both for the reputation of England and for her future relations with the Sikh people that the provocation and the attack came from Lahore and not from Calcutta. In the splendid record of the English conquest of India, illumined by so many chivalrous and noble actions, so much temperance in the hour of victory and so much generosity to the vanquished, there are still some episodes which, however pardonable in rough times, cannot be regarded by the impartial historian with approval. But the annexation of the Punjab is not one of these. It was accepted by the whole Sikh nation as just, and their acknowledged bravery in both campaigns and the loss they inflicted on their opponents, took the sting from defeat and left them the most loyal subjects the Queen has in the East. Their devotion and their gallantry have been proved many times, and if they continue to be governed as wisely and sympathetically as in the early years succeeding annexation, they will remain, what they now are, the sword and shield of British India.

CHAPTER II

The Sikhs

The Sikh people, mostly of Ját descent, are roughly divided into two great classes, named from the districts they inhabit, the Mánjha and the Málwá, and the origin and history of these are altogether different. The Mánjha is the name of the southern portion of the Bári Doáb (the word doáb signifying a tract of country between two rivers, here the Beas and the Rávi), in the neighbourhood of the cities of Lahore and Amritsar; and the Mánjha Sikhs, by a convenient enlargement of the terms, may be held to include all those who at the time of the final dissolution of the Muhammadan power, were resident to the north of the river Sutlej.

Málwá is the country immediately to the south of the same river [1], stretching towards Delhi and Bíkaner, and the Sikhs who inhabit this district, being the original settlers and not mere invaders or immigrants from the Mánjha, are known as the Málwá Sikhs. Their acknowledged head is the great Phúlkian house, of

[1] Not to be confused with Málwá of the Deccan; the rich country north of the Narbadá, of which Indore is the centre.

which the Mahárájá of Patiála is the chief representative, with the closely allied families of Nábha, Jínd Bhadour, Malod, Badrúkan, Jiundan, Diálpúra Landgharia, Rámpúr and Kot Dhúna, with the more distantly connected houses of Farídkot and Kythal.

The ancestors of the Málwá Sikhs were simple Hindu peasants, mostly of Rájput extraction, who about the middle of the sixteenth century emigrated from the neighbourhood of Jaisalmer, and settled as peaceful subjects of the Muhammadan rulers of Delhi. In the course of a hundred years, as the central authority grew weak, the power of the Ját settlers increased. They were *málguzárs* or payers of revenue into the imperial treasury, and made no efforts to shake off a yoke which was in no way galling; but they acquired large grants of land, founded villages, and became wealthy and of some social importance. But about the beginning of the eighteenth century, the Málwá chiefs abandoned Hinduism for the new faith which was then being preached by Govind, the last and the most influential of the Sikh Gurus. The hundred years that followed was a time of anarchy. The great Muhammadan Empire was, from inherent weakness, falling asunder, and the Sikhs day by day gained power and territory at the expense of their nominal masters, who persecuted the new faith but were unable to destroy it. Sikhism was then, as Muhammadanism in the seventh and eighth centuries, and Wahabeeism in the present, a religion of the sword, and the new converts appeared as ready to fight with each other as with the common enemy against whom alone they ever united. The Sikhs did not avowedly abandon the Hindu codes of law which they had from time immemorial obeyed, and neither Nának nor Govind laid down new rules by which their followers should be bound in matters of marriage and inheritance, but they felt a contempt for Hinduism with its restrictions and prejudices, and refused to follow its precepts whenever they were opposed to their immediate interests. Society was in a state of demoralisation. Each man did what was right in his own eyes, and whatever he could do with impunity appeared to him right. Widows and orphans had no helper against the powerful neighbours who divided their lands amongst them at their pleasure; and the only means by which the smaller chiefs could escape absorption was by attaching themselves as feudal retainers or vassals to the great houses, who were able and willing to protect them in return for service in the field. Thus arose the great Cis-Sutlej chiefs, whose obscure origin and unprincipled acquisitions were ennobled by titles extorted from the Emperor of Delhi, who was still the nominal ruler of the Málwá, and was too weak and timid to refuse to honour the men whom he knew to be the most formidable enemies of his power.

At the beginning of the present century the fate which the Cis-Sutlej chiefs had so often brought upon others seemed likely to become their own. Ranjít Singh, Mahárájá of Lahore, having reduced to submission the chiefs in the neighbourhood of his capital, determined to conquer the whole country to the south of the Sutlej, as far as the river Jumna, which, he believed, he might safely accomplish, without coming into collision with the English power. The condition of the Cis-Sutlej States eminently favoured the success of his design. Jealous of each other, and with no common bond of union now that the Muhammadan power had finally collapsed, they would, one by one, have fallen victims to the energy and determination of Ranjít Singh, whose ambition knew no limits and scruples, and to whom the very names of honour and pity were unknown. The Málwá chiefs saw their danger in time, and at the very moment when their annihilation seemed inevitable, threw themselves on the mercy of the British Government, which, after much hesitation, accepted the position and declared the Cis-Sutlej territory under its protection.

Then followed a period of unbroken security, during which the strong power which prevented any attack from without insisted upon tranquillity within, and maintained the smallest as well as the largest States in the possession of the dignity and power which they had possessed when first they claimed its protection. It was during this period that the rules of succession became, to a certain degree, uniform and consistent, although it will be understood that these are but comparative terms when applied to laws that prevailed in a society so exceptionally constituted, which had learned so lately the advantages of order, and which had been accustomed for so long to consider license synonymous with liberty.

The effect of the Sutlej campaign of 1845-46 was almost precisely similar to that caused by the campaign of 1866 in Northern Germany. The British Government, which had for years deplored a state of things which it was unable without breaking faith with the chiefs to rectify, which had seen the people oppressed and ground down by petty tyrants who possessed absolute power in their respective States, seized the opportunity which the folly and ingratitude of the chiefs had given to inaugurate a new order of things. The most important chiefs alone were permitted to retain their power, while that of the smaller ones was taken altogether away: they were declared mere *Jagírdárs* of the British Government, and the whole of their territories was placed under the control of British Officers and British Courts of Law.

It will thus appear that the Málwá chiefs have passed through several distinct periods of development. First, the mere cultivators of the lands on which, as immigrants, they had settled; then, the owners of those same lands. Next came the period of conflict with the Muhammadan power, during which the chiefships grew up gradually and naturally, followed by the period of tranquillity which was the consequence of their claiming British protection. The last period saw the majority of them stripped of the power which they had infamously abused, and which it was a misfortune to the country that they had ever possessed.

There is no gradual development such as this to be traced in the history of the Sikh chiefs of the Mánjha. Scarcely more than a hundred years ago the majority of them were cultivators of the soil, enjoying none of the consideration which the Cis-Sutlej chiefs had, for long, received from the Court of Delhi. With the last invasions of Ahmad Sháh and the Afgháns, they rose to sudden power, and every man who had energy and courage gathered a band of marauders about him and plundered the country, seizing and holding whatever lands he could. Many of these Sikhs crossed the Sutlej and ravaged the country to the very gates of Delhi, while some of them seized large tracts of land Cis-Sutlej, which they continued to hold against all comers by the sword alone, a tenure altogether different from that of their Málwá neighbours, and more resembling that of a Norman baron settled in the Welsh marches seven hundred years ago.

The ascendency of the Sikhs in the Punjab Trans-Sutlej was but brief. Mahárájá Ranjít Singh subdued them one by one; Rámgarbias, Bhangis, Kanheyas; all the great houses fell in turn, and so completely that the chiefships became merely nominal, dependent on the will of the sovereign of Lahore.

The districts which contain the largest Sikh population—Ambála, Ludhiána, Jálandhar, Hoshiárpur, Amritsar, Lahore, Gurdáspur, Gujránwála, Siálkot, and Firozpur—are the most populous in the Punjab. For administrative purposes, the district is the political, fiscal and judicial unit, while several districts, ordinarily three in number, are grouped to form the more important administrative area known as a Division. The four Punjab divisions of Ambála, Jálandhar, Amritsar, and Lahore are those which include all the Sikh districts above given, and there is no reason to believe that there has been any large migration of Sikhs to or from other districts since the days of Ranjít Singh [1]. It may be that the presence of a great native court temporarily attracted to Lahore and Amritsar an exceptional number of Sikhs from a distance; while the absolute peace and security now enjoyed may have encouraged colonists to settle in localities and among a Muhammadan population where they would not have ventured fifty years ago to show their face. But, on the other hand, the Sikh population is mostly agricultural, and has little inclination to leave its hereditary holdings except for temporary service in the army. Thus it is that the distribution of the Sikh population will be found to be much the same at present as under Maháráját Ranjít Singh. What the total number of the Sikh population was in his day, and what proportion it bore to the general population of the whole Punjab, it is impossible to say, for no accurate statistics are available before the census of 1855. Other enumerations were made in 1868, 1881, and 1891, the figures of the latest not being yet available for purposes of com-

[1] See p. 8.

parison[1]. It will be interesting to ascertain whether the Sikhs are, as some believe and as the 1881 census seemed to indicate, diminishing in numbers, or whether the fluctuation was only accidental and temporary. There are obviously many considerations which influence the question. The Sikh represents a creed, not a race. Of the Hindu, of whatever caste, it may be said, as of the poet, *nascitur non fit.* His birth status is unalterable. But with the Sikh the exact reverse is the case. Born of a Sikh father, he is not himself counted of the faith until, as a grown boy, he has been initiated and received the baptism of the *páhul* at the Akál Bungah or some equally sacred place. Thus the supply of candidates for baptism is apt to rise or fall with the popular estimate of the advantages or disadvantages of joining the communion. During the days of Ranjít Singh, when spiritual fervour and national pride worked in common, the numbers who joined the dominant faith were proportionally great. At the time of the first British census of 1855 the outside influences were depressing. The Khálsa had fallen to rise no more, and its members were uncertain of the temper of their new masters, who might be expected to be angry with those who had forced upon them the burthen and expense of two wars. As a consequence the Sikhs lay low and did not bring their sons to baptism. It

[1] The Census Report of the Punjab for 1881 was compiled by Mr. Denzil Ibbetson of the Civil Service. It is a work of the highest ability and interest, and a treasure-house of valuable facts regarding the social history and development of the province.

was as well to wait and watch events, and the *páhul* can be taken at any period of life.

When the census of 1868 was taken, there had been a great and welcome change. The Mutiny had taken place, and the Sikhs had cordially joined their conquerors in reestablishing order in Hindustán. Their share had been an especially grateful and glorious one. Perhaps a more fortunate occurrence than the Mutiny of 1857 never occurred in India. It swept the Indian sky clear of many clouds. It disbanded a lazy, pampered army, which, though in its hundred years of life it had done splendid service, had become impossible; it replaced an unprogressive, selfish and commercial system of administration by one liberal and enlightened; and it attached the Sikh people closely to their rulers and made them, what they are to-day, the surest support of the Government. Lastly, it taught India and the world that the English possessed a courage and national spirit which made light of disaster; which never counted whether the odds against them were two or ten to one; and which marched confident to victory, although the conditions of success appeared all but hopeless. After the Mutiny the Sikhs found themselves no longer regarded with suspicion by their new masters, but treated in a spirit of confidence and good fellowship. The name of Sikh became what it was in the days of the great Mahárájá, a title of honour opening to its possessor the door of military service. Thus the creed received a new impulse, and many sons of Sikhs, whose baptism had been deferred, received the *páhul*, while new candidates from among the Játs and lower caste Hindus joined the faith.

Since those days of enthusiasm a natural reaction has set in, and comparing the census of 1881 with that of 1868 there appears to be a falling off in almost all the central districts. This is in part due to inconsistency in the returns, and an erroneous inclusion of the Nánaki Sikhs, who do not adopt the surname of Singh, with the followers of the tenth Guru Govind. But the chief reason is found in the strong attractive force of Hinduism, which, in days of peace, when martial instincts have less influence, retains its hold of the people. Its ivy-like vitality, enfolding and strangling everything which it has once grasped, has been fatal to almost all creeds which, like Sikhism and Buddhism, both heterodox forms of Hinduism, have put themselves in competition with it. As the Church of Rome in the West so is Hinduism in the East. When it has ebbed like the tide and its enemies have believed in a victory, it has returned on the flood in all its former strength. Hinduism has been ever hostile to Sikhism, for the latter faith attacked it in its most vital principle of caste, without which the whole Bráhmanical system falls to the ground. The influence of Hinduism on Sikhism is doubly felt, both in preventing the children of Sikh fathers from taking the *páhul*, and by indirectly withdrawing professed Sikhs from the faith. The performance of a few expiatory rites, the payment of a certain sum of money to the Bráhmans, the disuse of the militant surname, and the Sikh reverts, as a Ját peasant, into the ordinary Hindu community. Even where there has been no abandonment of the Sikh name and creed the tendency is always, in less essential matters, to revert to the practice of the ancient religion, and it is here, as in all countries, that feminine influence is paramount.

To women, altogether uneducated, the abstract faith of Sikhism, whether the philosophical theism of Nának or the political teaching of Govind Singh, is far less attractive than the Hindu polytheism, which is easy to be understood and which gives to their religious exercises a colour and life that the dry recital of obscure passages of the *Granth* cannot impart. Joining in the Hindu worship, the women have their share in the outdoor life of their sisters in the village. The morning visit to the temple, or to the stones stained with red ochre where the protecting deity of the community resides; the numerous festivals of the Hindu pantheon, with the noise and excitement and fine clothes; these are the only diversions of native women, whose lives are ordinarily sad and monotonous, and whose only dissipations are religious. To choose between Hinduism and Sikhism was for them as if English women were asked to choose between a ball-room and a Quaker meeting. Moreover, the influence of the priest, whether a Catholic or a Bráhman, weighs more heavily on the woman than on the man. She is dependent on the priest for a good deal of her happiness in this world and for her safety in the next. The Bráhman and the soothsayer promise her children, that no strange new wife shall take away her husband's love, and that the proper observance of Hindu ritual will secure her good fortune hereafter. The men are not exempt from the influence of the same sentiments. The old tradition of Bráhmanism is too strong for the new reforming creed to resist. The result is that the old order returns; the Sikh, although he will not smoke or cut his hair or beard, pays reverence to Bráhmans, and visits the temples and shrines of the old faith, and observes the superstitious practices of other Hindus. In the matter of caste the Sikh retains a large part of his freedom, and will drink or eat food from the vessels of a Christian or a Muhammadan should necessity require it. At no time has he been accustomed to associate with what the Hindus account as unclean castes; and the sweepers or Mazbi Sikhs, who are very numerous (for Sikhism was naturally very attractive to the lowest castes), have been always excluded from the Sikh shrines, and the British Government has been compelled to form them into separate regiments, when they have fought quite as gallantly as their better-born co-religionists.

Even in the palmiest days of the Khálsa it is astonishing how small a proportion of the Punjab population was of the Sikh profession. The fierce fanaticism of the earlier years of the century was succeeded by the unequalled military organisation of the Mahárájá, and these together enabled a people who were never numerically more than a sect of Hinduism to overrun the whole Punjab and Kashmír, to beat back the Afgháns to the mountains, and to found a powerful kingdom in which they were outnumbered by Hindus and Muhammadans by ten to one.

The population of the Punjab, exclusive of Kashmír, was, by the census of 1881, 22,712,120, of which 11,662,434 were Muhammadans, 9,232,295 Hindus, and 1,716,114 Sikhs. Taking British territory only, there is to each 10,000 of the general population of the Punjab a proportion of 595 Sikhs, being 55 per 10,000 less than in the census of 1868, when the proportion was 650. The districts in which Sikhs are proportionally most numerous are Firozpur, where they make 2595 out of each 10,000 of the population; Amritsar, where they make 2422; and Ludhiána, where they make 2055. Although the Sikhs may have been proportionally more numerous in the time of Ranjít, yet it is probable that they were more concentrated in the central districts, and in the most prosperous days of the Khálsa they never exceeded a total of two millions [1].

The Native States absorb more than a third of the total Sikh population of the Punjab, Patiála naturally taking the first place, the proportion to the general population being 2781 per 10,000. The distribution of the Sikhs according to caste is a

[1] A telegram from India of the 7th Feb. 1892 gives the Sikh population by the census of 1891 as 1,907,836 for the whole continent.

highly interesting question which, until the last census, was never worked out with any exactness. It now appears that of 1000 Sikhs in the several administrative divisions of the province, an average of 699 belong to the agricultural castes, Játs, Rájputs, Sainis, and Kambohs, the proportion being highest in the districts south of the Sutlej. Of the mercantile castes, Aroras, Banyás, and Khattrís are 47 per 1000. Of the artisan castes, potters, weavers, blacksmiths, carpenters, goldsmiths, barbers, and the like, 134 per 1000, and the menial and outcaste groups include 95. The artisan Sikhs are distributed very evenly in all districts, but the mercantile Sikhs are almost exclusively found in the Mussulman districts, in some of which, the Ráwal Pindi Division for example, they form a majority of the Sikh population. The religious castes, Bráhmans and Fakírs, are hardly represented at all, only 4 per 1000 of the Punjab Sikhs belonging to the priestly class.

The backbone of the Sikh people is the great Ját caste which, divided and subdivided into numerous clans and tribes, is by far the most important of all the Punjab races. The origin of the Játs is shrouded in much uncertainty, and has been the subject of long discussion. Some distinguished writers have found for them a Getic origin, but the traditions of the Punjab Játs, in almost all cases, refer to a Rájput descent and emigration to the Punjab from Central India. Even the Sindhu and Waraich Játs, who claim a Trans-Indus origin, are by no means unanimous, and portions of both tribes refer to Rájputána as their ancient home. And in no instance is there a record of any tribe emigration from the west of the Indus, the founders of both Sindhus and Waraichs being spoken of as solitary emigrants. There seems nothing in the language of the Punjab Játs to favour the theory of Getic descent. My own researches into the subject, which at one time were extensive, led me to the belief, which is shared by Mr. Ibbetson, the author of the Census Report, that the Játs and Rájputs are generally derived from a common stock, and that the present distinction is rather social than ethnic. The Játs outnumber the Rájputs by three to one, and from every point of view, their military worth, their excellence as agriculturists, their industry, honesty, and tractability, they are the most important and valuable of the Punjab races. The Játs are thoroughly independent in character, and assert personal and individual freedom as against communal or tribal control more strongly than any other people. But although ready to fight on occasion, they are not of a cruel or vindictive disposition, and make good citizens in times of peace and form the solid, tax-paying community, as they are the most successful, patient, and enduring cultivators. They hold a social place below the Bráhman, the Rájput, and the Khattrí, but they themselves assert an equality with the second and a superiority over the third of these castes, a claim which their historical record and present importance justify. They are seen at their best in the Sikh districts about the rivers Beas and Sutlej. In the southern and frontier districts they show altogether different characteristics, and have, in many cases, a different and non-Rájput origin.

The virtues of the Játs are thus identical with those of the Sikhs who have come out of this caste, while the new creed has added a more ardent military spirit which is the principal tradition of the creed and which it should be the earnest desire of the British Government to maintain. As the English power in India becomes more consolidated and resistance to its authority grows each year less common, it must result that the fighting races will have less opportunity for gratifying their martial instincts. The soldier everywhere gives way to the husbandman; the sword is beaten into a ploughshare, and we are disposed to boast of the universal *Pax Britannica* as if all administrative triumphs were bounded by and included in peace. But for an Empire like India, of 288 millions, which has many dangers from without and enemies ever ready to pierce the weak places in her armour, war is necessary to healthy life. The sword must be always sharp and must not be left too long rusting in the scabbard. If the rulers of India be wise, they will in every way encourage and stimulate the military spirit of the Sikhs and employ them on active service on every opportunity, whether the campaign be in Europe, Asia, or Africa. The all important thing is to give them the highest and most varied military training against every class of foe,

European as well as Asiatic. The numbers of the home army of England are so small, and its organisation so faulty and inelastic, that India must obviously be prepared to defend herself against attack from without, and for this defence the fighting population of the Punjab, and notably the Sikhs, will be sufficient if reserves are formed in time and if the military spirit of the people is not allowed to fall asleep.

It is no use to expect from the Sikh more than he can give. His value to the British Government was shown in the Mutiny, when the Rájás of the Trans- and Cis-Sutlej, Patiála, Nábha, Jínd and Kapúrthala, on the very first alarm and without waiting to discover whether the omens were auspicious or hostile, placed themselves at the head of their troops and marched to Delhi to fight against the enemies of the English Government. Their gallant example was followed by the Sikh people throughout the province, and India was recovered for the Queen as much by the loyalty and devotion of her Punjab subjects as by the bayonets of her English soldiers. But the Sikh is not of much value in the office or the municipal committee, as will be hereafter shown when the practice of Ranjít Singh in the choice of his ministers is described. In school and college he is outstripped by students of almost all other races. But academic success is not, in the East, a test of fitness for high office. The smooth-tongued, supple Bengali would probably rank first in such a competition, although he has neither the physical courage to fight nor the moral courage to govern. And those who would undervalue the Ját Sikh as a useful citizen of the Empire, because his hereditary instincts and training disincline him to learning, would make a great mistake. The Sikh is a fighting man, and his fine qualities are best shown in the army, which is his natural profession. Hardy, brave, and of intelligence too slow to understand when he is beaten, obedient to discipline, devotedly attached to his officers, and careless of the caste prohibitions which render so many Hindu troops difficult to control and to feed on active service, he is unsurpassed as a soldier in the East. There are many warlike races, subjects of the Queen in India, and of these the Sikhs indisputably take the first place as thoroughly reliable, useful soldiers. The Gúrkhas are equally brave and enthusiastic in action, but they unfortunately are few in number, and do not for the most part inhabit British territory. They are mostly Nepálís, and conditions sometimes arise when it is very difficult to obtain high-class and sufficient recruits.

The Rájputs are excellent soldiers, though they have not the solidity of the Sikh. But the high-class Rájput is difficult to procure, and those who come into our service are mostly the half-bred Dogras of the hills, upon whom the Rájputs of the pure blood from Central India look down. Nor will these splendid men join our army until some system be devised of giving them officers of their own race. The Punjábi Muhammadans, Ghakkars, Awáns, Tiwánas are gallant soldiers; so are the Afghán clansmen from the North-

West frontier. But they are apt to get sadly home-sick if they are long on active service, and it is impossible to persuade many of them to leave the frontier. The children of the mountains are too free and independent to bear with any patience the restraints of civilization. But the Sikh is always the same; in peace, in war, in barracks or in the field, ever genial, good-tempered and uncomplaining: a fair horseman, a stubborn infantry soldier, as steady under fire as he is eager for a charge. The Sikhs, alone of our native troops, can be taken in large numbers and for long periods on foreign service, on the condition that they be well paid, for they have as keen a knowledge of the value of money, and as great a love of saving as the Scotch. They have served in Egypt, Abyssinia, Afghánistán, and China with great distinction; they have voluntarily taken service in the police and in local corps in Burma, a country which is especially distasteful to ordinary natives of India, and there is a local corps of Sikh police in Hong-Kong, where they are regarded with much confidence and respect. A Sikh escort is now with Mr. H. Johnston, the British Agent-General, fighting Arab slavers on Lake Nyassa. It is difficult to realize that the dignified, sober, and orderly men who now fill our regiments are of the same stock as the savage freebooters whose name, a hundred years ago, was the terror of Northern India. But the change has been wrought by strong and kindly government and by strict military discipline under sympathetic officers whom the troops love and respect. I had many opportunities of observing the conduct of the Sikh troops during the latter portion of the campaign in Afghánistán, and no praise could be too high for their patience under privation and their admirable and orderly behaviour towards the Afgháns, who it must be remembered were their bitter and ancient enemies.

What may be their value against European troops is a question which the future alone can authoritatively decide; but I would venture to express my conviction, which is shared by many distinguished officers of the Indian army, that the Sikhs, infantry and light cavalry, are, when well and sufficiently led by English officers, equal to any troops in the world, and superior to any with whom they are likely to come in contact.

CHAPTER III

The Sikh Theocracy

Mahárájá Ranjít Singh was so completely a product of the Sikh theocracy, and so embodied the spirit of the Khálsa, that no account of his character and career would be complete without a description of the religious system which had so powerful an effect upon the Ját cultivators of the Punjab in the eighteenth and the first half of the nineteenth century. The subject is too extensive and complicated to be treated here in a detailed or even a satisfactory fashion, and I would invite those who desire to be fully informed of the nature of Sikh dogmata and ethics to study the translation of the *Ádi Granth* or the Holy Scriptures of the Sikhs, translated from the original Gúrmukhi, with introductory essays, by Dr. Ernest Trumpp, Regius Professor of Oriental languages at the University of Munich, who, in 1870, was entrusted by the Secretary of State with this important work. I happened to be Chief Secretary to Government at Lahore when Dr. Trumpp was engaged on this duty, of which the extreme difficulty was only equalled by his zeal, industry and learning. He found that the Sikh priests and *Granthís* (readers and expounders of the scriptures) were marvellously ignorant of the principles of their own religion; that they had no knowledge of the old Gúrmukhi forms or idioms. Their explanations of doubtful passages were only traditional, and conflicted with other parts of the sacred volume, and it was only after procuring some scarce commentaries, very imperfect and almost as obscure as the original text, that Dr. Trumpp managed to accomplish the work. Before he could do so he had to compile a dictionary and a grammar of the *Granth*, containing all Gúrmukhi forms and obsolete words. The difficulties in the way of the completion of his task seemed almost insuperable, and at last the learned Professor, in spite of my urgent remonstrances, fled from Lahore to Germany, where, after seven years' labour, he produced a translation which, although it will never attract the general reader, is still a monument of industry and learning. Previous accounts of the religion of the Sikhs, such as those contained in the works of Captain Joseph Cunningham and Mr. H. H. Wilson in his sketch of the religious sects of the Hindus, are slight and defective, for the reason that the writers were not acquainted with the Sikh scriptures or the commentaries upon them; nor is it easy even now to follow the thin thread of doctrine running through the involved, incoherent and shallow pages of the *Ádi Granth*. These are filled with inconsistent trivialities and vain repetitions, although there are some portions, especially the Slóks of the Bhagats Kabír and Faríd, which are added as an appendix to the *Granth* itself, which contain passages of great picturesqueness and beauty, and which, although not poetry in the technical sense of the word, still have many of its attributes. They resemble strongly, and compare favourably with, the writings of Walt Whitman, the American poet.

The *Ádi Granth* derives its chief authority from Bábá Nának, the founder of the religious system of the Sikhs, who wrote large portions of it about the beginning of the seventeenth century. It was collected in its present state by Arjun, the fifth of the Gurus or Sikh prophets, who added to the writings of Nának those of his successors and of other older mystical Hindu authors. More important than the *Ádi Granth*, as determining the military and political constitution of later Sikhdom, were the writings of the tenth and greatest of the Sikh Gurus, Govind Singh, who, in 1696, composed a voluminous work, partly by his own hand and partly by the aid of Hindi poets attached to him, teaching, in archaic and exceedingly difficult Hindi, the tenets of the new faith which he preached. Guru Govind Singh did not however change the esoteric doctrine of Nának in any essential particulars, although his teaching and practice were more distinctly pantheistic. He was himself a worshipper of the goddess Dúrga and allowed adoration of the inferior divinities of the Hindu Pantheon, although he preferentially advocated the worship of the one Supreme God.

The limits of space do not permit of telling in any detail the story of the lives of the ten Sikh Gurus, and what is necessary to say regarding them must be compressed into a few pages.

Nának, the founder of the religion, whose most authentic *Janam Sákhi* or biography was unearthed by Dr. Trumpp in the library of the India Office, to which it had been presented by the illustrious H. T. Colebrooke, was born in the year 1469, at a village called Talwandi[1] on the bank of the Rávi, near the city of Lahore. He was one of the Khattrí or trading class, and filled the respectable village office of *patwári* or accountant. Regarding his childhood and youth, the miraculous stories which congeal around the founder of every successful religion are told. He appears to have lived a commonplace life, to have married and had children. Going one day to bathe in the river, he was taken up by angels and carried to the Divine Presence where he received the gift of prophecy and orders to preach the doctrine of the true God on earth. In obedience to this divine mission, Nának abandoned wife and family, and with one follower, named Mardána, he assumed the garb of an ascetic and roamed about the world preaching the new faith. The Sikh biographies give accounts of his wanderings to the north, south, east and west, and to a romantic country, called Gorak Hatari, a kind of Indian Utopia; but during these journeys, filled with incredible marvels, no events of much importance are recorded except the interview of the prophet with the Emperor Bábar, who is described as receiving

[1] Afterwards called Nánkhána in honour of the Guru.

Nának with kindness and courtesy, which is likely enough from all we know of that genial and illustrious monarch. Towards the close of his life Nának returned to his family at Kartárpur in Jálandhar, where he died in 1538. His life had been uneventful, much resembling that of any other Hindu fakír, and the influence he left behind him was enshrined in his writings which were subsequently collected. He named as his successor, passing over his two sons, his disciple Angad. The word *Sikhs*, literally learners, disciples, was given to his followers by Nának, and as the creed spread, became the descriptive title of the whole people; but it must be remembered that the term Sikh is a religious and not a racial designation, and belongs only to those of the faith of the Khálsa.

Arjun, the fifth Guru, collected the writings of Nának, together with extracts from the works of popular saints and poets, into one volume, recorded, not in Sanskrit, like the Vedas and Puránas of Hinduism, and consequently not understood by the people, but in the Punjábi dialect, which was the popular tongue. Not that the whole of the *Ádi Granth* is written in the same style. Its idiom varies according to the time and place of the contributions. Its value as a treasury of old Hindi dialects is immense. The idiom of Bábá Nának and his successors is not the pure Punjábi as then spoken, which is found in the *Janam Sákhi* of Nának, but contains a large admixture of old Hindi forms and words, the intention being to raise the dialect into something more stately than the colloquial idiom, while, at the same time, retaining the power of being popularly understood. The writings of Guru Govind Singh are composed in almost pure Hindi, and as such are at the present day unintelligible to the Punjábi-speaking Sikhs.

The most important chapter of the *Ádi Granth* is the first, known as Jápu or Jápji, which was written by Nának himself and contains an exposition of doctrine, while, as a literary effort, it is superior to anything in the volume, except, perhaps, some of the mystical writings of Kabír or Shekh Faríd to which reference has already been made. The reputation of the Bhagat Kabír is widely spread in India, and there is still a monastery of his disciples, the Kabír-panthís, at Benares, where his writings are expounded [1]. The earliest composers whose writings are included in the *Granth* are two Maráthí poets, Nám Deva and Trilokan, whose peculiar dialects, akin to the modern Maráthí in many of its forms, prove their birthplace to have been in the Deccan.

Govind Singh, the tenth and last of the Gurus, was fifteen years old when his father was tortured and killed as a martyr by the bigoted Emperor Aurangzeb. The boy fled to the hills where he remained for some years completing his education, in which he was superior to his predecessors, knowing Persian, Hindi and a little Sanskrit, which he at times attempted to introduce into his later compositions.

[1] Guru Govind, Sákhi 98, warmly praised Kabír as a devotee, near to God and superior to kings, whose memory would remain fresh through the ages.

It does not appear that this remarkable man, who, in intelligence, capacity, and fixed purpose was infinitely the superior of all his predecessors, undertook what he considered to be the mission of his life, in the formation of the scattered Sikh people into a formidable confederacy and the destruction of the Muhammadan power in the Punjab, until he was well advanced in manhood; certainly over thirty years of age. Till then he devoted himself to study and a preparation for his self-imposed duties. At the same time, not neglecting the accomplishments of a well-born youth of his age, he became a keen sportsman and skilled in all feats of arms. When he emerged from seclusion he was at once accepted by the Sikh people as their natural and hereditary leader, and they were quite ready to follow him to avenge the murder of his father on their Muhammadan oppressors. Before commencing his work he desired to obtain the blessing of the Hindu goddess Dúrga, whose shrine on the hill of Naina Devi was near his home at Anandpur. After the practice of the necessary preliminary austerities, numerous and long continued, and the presentation of milk, clarified butter and grain, the goddess appeared and demanded a human sacrifice as the price of her protection; and the priests told him that the most acceptable offering would be the head of one of his four sons. The mothers of the children naturally refused to surrender them to such a fate, and Govind Singh then turned to his friends, of whom it is recorded that five offered themselves as the sacrifice, and one, whose name is not given, was accepted and slain before the shrine. There is little doubt, in spite of discrepancies in the story, that this human sacrifice was offered up. In old days this bloodthirsty goddess, under various forms and names, demanded frequent human victims, and it is only since the British Government has declined to allow the alliance of religion with murder, that goats instead of men are slain on her altars. The goddess approved the offering, and the subsequent career of Govind Singh and his violent death seemed foreshadowed in its bloody inauguration. The Guru now assembled his followers, and, assured of the sacred character of his mission and its success, began boldly to preach the new doctrine which was to supersede that of Nának as a political creed and unite the Sikhs, in the manner which Arjun and Har Govind had suggested, into a military nation. The old Sikh faith had a baptismal rite which had fallen into disuse. This was resuscitated by Govind Singh as the necessary initiatory ceremony of Sikhism. The *páhul* he administered to all his disciples present. The procedure was by the dissolution of sugar-candy in pure water which was stirred by a dagger. Over this certain verses from the Japji of the *Granth* were recited and the neophyte drank a portion, the rest being sprinkled on his head and body, while the baptizer and the disciple shouted '*Wah! Guruji ka Khálsa*' (Victory to the Khálsa of the Guru)[1].

[1] The name of the new Sikh Commonwealth, the *Khálsa*, is,

After Guru Govind had baptized his five disciples, a number significant in the Khálsa as forming a special congregation in which the Guru promised that his spirit should be ever present, he caused them to administer to him the same initiatory rite, taking the title of Singh, which was enjoined to be added as a baptismal name to all new professors of the faith. In the present day the Singhs are the only Sikhs who are accepted as such in popular estimation, and the Nánaki Sikhs are considered to have lapsed into the body of the Hindu population.

Govind Singh's next step was to adapt the Sikh scriptures to his own views, and with this object he endeavoured to induce the guardians of the *Ádi Granth* at the sacred city of Kartárpur to permit him to make additions to it; but the Sodhis, the Sikh priests who had the guardianship of the sacred volume and who were the descendants of Guru Rám Dás, refused to accept the authority of the new leader. They, with their great establishments at Anandpur and Kartárpur, had already become the Bráhmans of the Sikh creed, with the unbounded spiritual pride of their prototypes, and when they understood that the object of Govind Singh was to preach the democratic doctrine of equality in a far more liberal fashion than it had been promulgated by Nának himself, and that the lowest classes and even outcasts were to be admitted equally with Bráhmans to the higher privileges of the

according to Dr. Trumpp and contrary to the received derivation derived from the Arabic *Khálsah*, signifying one's own property, hence the Guru's or God's own special property.

Khálsa, they were in immediate revolt. They denounced Govind Singh as an impostor and refused to allow him to add his heterodox teaching to the sacred volume in their charge. They told him that if he were a true Guru he should compile scriptures for himself, which he at once proceeded to do, the work being completed in the year 1696. The object of Govind in this compilation was not to overturn or indeed to modify in any important particulars the doctrine bequeathed by Nának, but to produce a work which should have on his excitable and fanatical followers the effect which he desired in launching them as a militant power against the Muhammadans, and recovering the Punjab for the new congregation of the faithful. In this he was partly successful, and at the head of a continually increasing band of devoted followers, he commenced his life-work of propagating the true faith[1]. His first quarrels were with the Rájput chiefs of the Kángra Hills, who assembled their forces to attack him at Anandpur. In one of the fights which ensued near the village of Chamkour, now a place of pilgrimage, his two eldest sons, Ajit Singh and Johar Singh, were killed. The imperial troops had come to the assistance of the Rájputs, and drove the Guru from Anandpur and Machíwára successively, his two remaining sons being captured.

[1] A valued friend of mine, Sirdár Attar Singh of Bhadour, the head of one of the first Cis-Sutlej families, has translated and published an interesting collection of Sákhis, describing the wanderings and adventures of Guru Tegh Bahádur and his son Guru Govind Singh.

The children were taken to Sirhind, and there, by order of the Emperor Aurangzeb, were buried alive. The Guru continued his flight into the deserts south of the Sutlej [1], and after many adventures settled at Talwandi in Patiála territory, which he declared should be as sacred to the Sikhs as Benares to the Hindus. This halting place is known as Damdama (*dam*, breath), and is a great Sikh centre, the best Gúrmukhi writers being found here. Another town, Bhattinda, in the same State, is also known as a Damdama of the Guru. Here he expelled a demon which was wont to ravage the town, and remained in the neighbourhood for some time, his fame and influence continually increasing [2].

An interesting account of his life at this place is given in the Sákhis, which, with certain deductions for religious extravagance, may be accepted as a fairly accurate picture of the Sikh prophet holding court like a monarch, and attaching followers by his liberality and munificence. Nor were the credentials of the true prophet, by the working of miracles, absent. The Sákhis are full of the wonder-working power of the Guru. We find his blessing giving children to childless parents [3], expelling demons [4], banishing disease from a village [5], making brackish water sweet [6], punishing treachery by inflicting a deadly and hereditary disease [7], making a dead tree to bear leaves and blossoms [8]. On one occasion the Hindu and Muhamma-

[1] Sákhi, 53, 54, 55, of the wanderings of Guru Govind Singh.
[2] Sákhi, 86. [3] Sákhi, 8. [4] Sákhi, 86. 16.
[5] Sákhi, 5. [6] Sákhi, 2. [7] Sákhi, 50. [8] Sákhi, 10.

dan thieves who attempted to steal his horses were smitten with blindness [1], and on another he made a surveyor, who had been sent to appraise the crops of one of the faithful, so forgetful of his arithmetic that he acknowledged the Guru's authority and became a Sikh [2].

The magnificence of Govind Singh was not maintained without a great deal of oppression, and the Masands, or deputies of the Guru, took the place of the imperial tax-gatherers, and were so grasping and extortionate, and caused so much discontent and resistance, that he was compelled to abolish them altogether. He then returned to his home in Anandpur, passing Sirhind, which he with difficulty dissuaded his people from destroying in revenge for the cruel murder of his children. But he cursed the town, and ordered his followers whenever they passed it on pilgrimage to or from the Ganges to throw two bricks taken from its walls into the Sutlej or the Jumna, otherwise their bathing in the holy river would not profit them. This is still an invariable practice with the Sikhs who travel through the town on foot, though the railway has much reduced the number of such pilgrims. I have sometimes wandered through the ruins and mounds of rubbish which make up a great part of Sirhind, and have thought it a place which seemed truly accursed.

Some time after this, Govind Singh, for reasons which are obscure and which were certainly opposed

[1] Sákhi, 22. [2] Sákhi, 37.

to the tenour of his life and teaching, took service under the Emperor Bahádur Sháh; or perhaps it was no more than placing his services with a body of Sikh horse at the disposal of the Mussulman prince to divert suspicion from his generally rebellious conduct and secure a little respite from persecution. In any case he travelled, at the head of his followers, to the Deccan, where he was assassinated by the relatives of an Afghán, whom he had slain in a fit of anger. He died in 1708, at the age of forty-eight, at *Naderh*, on the river Godávari. This place is known by the Sikhs as *Abchalnagar*[1], where a shrine to his memory is annually visited by many Sikhs.

To understand the teaching of Govind a few words on the principles of the creed as expounded by Nának are necessary. First it may be observed that although the Sikhs revere the *Ádi Granth* as a direct revelation in the same degree as Christians and Muhammadans regard their respective scriptures, yet in the writings of Nának and his immediate successors, as collected by Guru Arjun, there is nothing which is of so novel and original a character as to deserve more attention than had been given by Punjábi Hindus to the teaching of holy men like Bhagat Kabír, from whom it would seem that Nának derived the greater part of his inspiration. The dogmas of the *Ádi Granth* differ in little from the esoteric teaching of Hinduism in its more ancient and purer forms. Nának was himself a mystic, and during a

[1] Abchalnagar, i. e. the town of the departure.

great part of his life an ascetic. His idea was not political like that of Govind Singh, but ethical, and he desired to raise Hinduism from the degraded forms of superstition and polytheism into which it had fallen and to preach, in addition to a nobler doctrine, a purer morality. He was a reformer in the best and truest sense of the word, and Sikhism, as expounded by him, in spite of the obscurity and extravagance which characterise the *Ádi Granth*, is a religion possessing a noble ideal and a practical and social meaning which place it very high among the philosophical religions of the civilized world.

There is much in the character and teaching of Nának which reminds the student of the life and teaching of the great Buddhist reformer, whose devotion to the cause of humanity and the general enlightenment of whose doctrine have had so vast an influence on a quarter of the human race.

The unity of the Supreme Being was the main point in the doctrine taught by Guru Nának; that He is One and Alone, as he affirms in the following couplet: 'Whom shall I call the second? There is none. In all there is that one Spotless One' (the Deity). The argument between Musulmans and Hindus on this particular point is also acknowledged where he says: 'Know that there are two ways (i.e. of Hindus and Muhammadans), but only one Lord.' The Deity, under whatever known name, as Brahm, Hari, Rám, or Govind, is incomprehensible, invisible, uncreated, eternal, and alone possessing any real existence. He is the root of all things; the Primary Cause from which all human beings and all Nature have been evolved; from whom everything has been expanded. In the same way as Darwin has taught the evolution of species, so did the doctrine of Nának proclaim, not the creation of Nature by the All-Powerful out of nothing, but the infinite division of His own essence into a plurality of forms. This doctrine is Pantheism, which in the *Granth* co-exists with an exalted Theism, sometimes one having greater prominence and sometimes the other, but on the whole it may be said that the teaching of the *Granth* is that the whole universe of animate and inanimate things is an emanation from the Divine Essence, who alone exists and without whom is no real or separate existence. Nature apart from God is a shadow, a delusion, and a mirage. At page 665 of the *Granth* it is said—

'1. The One is diffused in the many and all-filling; wherever I see, there is He.

'By the beautiful mirage of the Māya the world is deluded; only some rare one comprehends the truth.

'All is Govind, all is Govind, without Govind there is no other. As on one string there are seven thousand beads so is that Lord lengthwise and crosswise.

'2. A wave of water, froth and bubble, do not become separate from the water.

'This world is the sport of the Supreme Brahm playing about, He does not become another.'

The more theistic view of the *Granth* represents the Supreme Being as altogether distinct from the creatures he has made and which are an emanation from himself, unaffected by the universal Māya or delusion and resting uncontaminated by it, as the lotus flower remains distinct from the pool on which it rests. Polytheism is discountenanced and discredited in many parts in the *Granth*, when it takes the realistic form of idolatry; but Nának, in his teaching, did not directly denounce the polytheistic theory, and allowed the acceptance of the myriads of Hindu popular deities, all immeasurably inferior to the one Supreme Being, from whom, with all other things, they proceed. Nának taught that the great object of human exertion was to avoid transmigration, which is the principal object of apprehension by Hindus and Sikhs alike.

The Hindu doctrine is that all earthly actions, good or evil, carry with them their own reward or punishment. Those who have been altogether virtuous are received into heaven where they remain until the merit has worked out. Then the saint returns to earth and is reborn as a man under the most favourable conditions, through which he passes in innumerable transmigrations, his future being again determined by his conduct. If his life has been vicious or worldly, he is thrown into purgatory from which, after long periods of punishment, he is reborn in animal forms, the most degraded of which are reserved for the greatest moral turpitude. After countless transmigrations he again becomes a man and is able by virtuous conduct gradually to work off his former daughter in marriage except for very large sums of money. In such cases the girl is considered as dead by her own family.

Daughters and their issue were in all cases held incompetent to inherit, as, if this had been allowed in a society in which girls were always married as soon as they reached puberty, estates would have passed out of the possession of the original family.

The practice of *Satí*, or widow-burning, was common in the case of chiefs of high degree, when the women were not allowed to claim their privilege of re-marriage, and it was often extended to the female servants and concubines of the deceased. When Mahárájá Ranjít Singh died one of his wives, Mahtab Devi, was burnt with him [1], and three ladies of his zenána of the rank of Ráni. On the funeral pile of his son, Mahárájá Kharak Singh, one of his *chadar dálna* wives, a beautiful woman named Isar Kour, was burnt. She was unwilling to be a *Satí*; and it is said that she was forced to burn by the minister Rájá Dhyán Singh. Two of the wives of Nao Nihál Singh, the grandson of Ranjít Singh, became *Satís*. The last two widow-burnings in the Punjab were remarkable as showing

[1] This lady was a Rájput, the natural daughter of Rájá Sansar Chand Katoch. The *Sati* was probably a voluntary one, for the proud Rájput women used to consider the disagreeable duty of burning themselves with their husbands a privilege attaching to their blue blood. When the handsome Rájá Suchet Singh, great uncle to the present Mahárájá of Kashmír, was killed at Lahore, his ten wives and the three hundred unmarried ladies of his zenána committed *Sati*, some at Lahore, 150 at Rámnagar, where his head was brought, and the others at Jammu or their own homes.

resolution of the spirit of man into the Divine Essence is acquired by calling upon the name of the Supreme Being, Hari, by those who have been properly received into the faith, whom the Guru has himself accepted as elect and to whom he has confided the secret of correctly invoking the Sacred Name. This initiation on the part of the Guru was however, in the true spirit of Calvinism, confined to the elect, those on whose forehead Destiny had written the decree of their emancipation. Such fatalistic doctrine was not dwelt upon, for the obvious reason that the power of the Guru would diminish in proportion as it was understood that he could not relieve his followers from the burden of destiny, and it was generally taught that by religious exercises and by patient reception of the teaching of the Guru, the heart would be inclined to righteousness and a choice would thus be allowed which might counteract the fatalistic decree which was supreme over human will. If the doctrine was in itself contradictory, it was no more so than the conflict in Calvinism between predestination and freewill, and merely represented the human yearning to escape from the inevitable necessity with which the whole constitution of the universe appeared to surround and overwhelm mankind.

The most important doctrine of the *Granth* is that of reverence and obedience to the Guru and respect to and worship of the saints. The practices of ablution, of giving alms, of abstinence from animal food are enjoined, while, as ethical teaching, evil speaking, unchastity, anger, covetousness, selfishness, and want of faith are especially denounced. Nának also taught that the position of the householder, as head of the family and engaged in the business of the world, was most honourable, and strongly discouraged the idea that any special virtue was to be gained by the ascetic life. That true religion consisted, not in outward ceremonial and the acceptance of the religious profession, but in the state of the heart, and that it was possible to meditate with advantage on spiritual things while engaged in the ordinary business of life without retreating to the wilderness or the seclusion of a monastery. It is true that several ascetic bodies of Sikhs, of whom the Udásis and the Akális are the most numerous, subsequently broke away from the teaching of Nának, but these have always been considered more or less unorthodox, and the Sikh religion, as taught both by Nának and Govind Singh, was eminently suited for practical life.

Although the *Ádi Granth* is hostile to Bráhmans and altogether ignores or denies their pretensions, Nának did not directly enjoin the abolition of caste. Yet his teaching was democratic and he admitted as his disciples people of all classes without distinction. The doctrine of Nának was almost identical with that of his successors, and no change of any religious or social importance was introduced until the time of Guru Govind Singh, whose teaching and book of conduct were a new starting-point for the Sikhs and did more than the authority of Nának to form them into the military nation which they afterwards became.

Govind Singh, although, as has been before stated, he was more inclined to polytheistic ideas than to the refined Pantheism of Nának, did not desire or find it convenient to attack the doctrine of his great predecessor, when the Sodhis of Anandpur sarcastically suggested his writing a new scripture for himself. What he wished was to consolidate the Sikh power, to bring the Sikhs more completely out of the ranks of Hinduism, so as to launch them with greater effect against Muhammadanism, and his first step was to abolish the custom of caste upon which Bráhmanism is founded. This naturally brought upon him the wrath of the priests of that creed and the dislike and suspicion of all the higher castes, whose immemorial privileges were abridged or destroyed by the admission into the Sikh body of those whom they most despised. This part of Nának's practice had been a stumbling-block to Hindu converts of the higher castes, but it was not made with him a matter of vital importance as with Govind Singh.

The other precepts of Govind Singh, with the object of separating his followers from the general body of Hindus, do not require lengthy notice; they were principally rules of conduct regarding dress, food and worship. The Sikhs were enjoined to wear blue garments, a practice which has long been discontinued, except in the case of the Akális; they were to carry a sword, and in addition five articles, the Punjábi names of which commence with the letter K. The *kes*, or uncut hair and beard; the *khanda*, or dagger; the *kanga*, or wooden comb; the *kára*, or iron bangle; and *kuchh*, short drawers coming to the knee. This last was to distinguish them from the Hindus, who invariably wear a loin cloth or *dhoti*, and they were further forbidden to smoke tobacco, a universal Hindu custom, and one, the prohibition of which it must have been difficult to enforce, and which has not had a favourable result. The Sikhs have largely taken to the consumption of opium and hemp, the latter of which is far more injurious than tobacco. The same prohibition has produced the same effect among the fanatical Muhammadans of Central Asia.

Female infanticide was prohibited, and they who killed their daughters were pronounced accursed. This custom in the time of Govind Singh and up to the British annexation of the Punjab was very prevalent, especially in the higher castes, such as the Rájputs, who had the greatest difficulty in disposing of their daughters. As an example may be mentioned the Rájput house to which Mahárájá Guláb Singh of Jammu belonged. Here the practice was invariable, and no marriage of a daughter was known to have taken place in that family until 1871, when the Mahárájá's granddaughter was married, amidst great rejoicings, to the son of the ancient house of Jaswal. In spite of the prohibition of Govind, the practice long remained common among the Sikhs, and even to-day there are parts of the Punjab where, especially in sacerdotal Sikh families, the practice is suspected to prevail; but as a rule it may be said that English influence has put an end to this cowardly and infamous crime throughout the Punjab. The practice of taking money for the hand of a daughter or sister was also forbidden; a prohibition which was often evaded.

The Sikhs were forbidden to eat meat killed in ordinary fashion, and animals for food were ordered to be slaughtered with one stroke of the sword. No special prohibition of beef is mentioned in the *Granth*, but the old tradition was too strong to be set aside, and the cow has remained as sacred an animal to the Sikh as to the ordinary Hindu. In frontier raids the vanquished Muhammadans would throw themselves at the feet of their conquerors, and putting a tuft of grass in their mouths, would appeal for quarter, crying out, 'I am your cow.' The Muhammadans were especially held accursed, and the prohibition against Sikhs wearing a cap was to dissociate them from the Muhammadans even in dress. War with these enemies of the faith was enjoined and no quarter was to be given to them. Unorthodox Sikhs, Jains and Jogis, were also declared accursed.

There were many minor prohibitions and directions, and one of the most important, the daily reading of the *Granth*, was impossible of practice for the reason that the Sikhs were commonly illiterate and were compelled to content themselves with occasionally attending to hear the *Granth* read by the lay priests,

Granthís, or reciting a passage which they had learned by heart.

No change took place in Sikh doctrine after the promulgation of Govind Singh's precepts, but as has been elsewhere shown, the practice grew more and more lax, till within recent years a new sect of reformers arose, founded originally by an Udási fakír of Ráwal Pindi. His successor, a carpenter of the Ludhiána district, named Rám Singh, rose to considerable importance and attached to himself a large number of fanatical disciples known as Kukas, who were distinguished by a peculiar dress and by secret watchwords and political organization.

The original movement was religious, an attempt to reform the Sikh practice and restore it to the character it possessed in the time of Govind Singh. As the sect grew in numbers, its ambition increased, till, at last, it preached a revival of the Khálsa and the downfall of the British Government. At this time I happened to be the Chief Secretary to the Punjab Government, and the proceedings of the Kukas caused a great amount of anxiety and trouble. They were not, however, in spite of their seditious teaching, interfered with until they broke into open revolt and attacked the Muhammadan town of Maler Kotla near Ludhiána. The insurrection was put down with great severity and some fifty of the rebels were blown from guns after summary trial. At the same time all the Kuka leaders in different districts of the Punjab were arrested in one night and deported, some to Rangoon, others to Aden, and the less important were confined in Punjab jails. The proceeding of the local authorities of the Ambála Division in blowing the rebels from guns was disapproved by the Punjab and Supreme Governments, as too drastic a remedy for the disorder. But, on the other hand, their action was taken in good faith, and there is much to be said in favour of the policy of suppressing rebellion in the swiftest and surest manner. It is, in any case, certain that the proceedings then taken were the death-blow to a formidable agitation against the Government. and the Kukas, although not extinct, have subsided into a disreputable sect whose communistic and debauched habits have brought upon them the general reprobation of the Sikh community.

In ordinary matters the Sikhs obeyed the Hindu law. But in some important particulars, notably in that of marriage, they had customs of their own which, in their turn, affected the rules of succession to property. The accepted rule was that, failing male heirs, the widow inherited the estate. But in wild times, when the sword was the only arbiter in disputes, and women were too weak to hold what had been won by the force and strength of men, the practice had grave inconveniences. The Sikh women had some of the virtues of their sex, and have on occasion shown themselves the equals of men in wisdom and administrative ability. Ráni Aus Kour of Patiála, Ráni Dya Kour of Ambála, and Mai Sada Kour, for long the head of the great Kanhoya confederacy, are examples of this. But, as a rule, an estate which fell into the hands of a Sikh widow was apt to be exploited by her lover for his personal advantage, till it would be seized by some one stronger and with as valid a claim to its possession. To avert this evil, the practice followed by the Jews in old times, of marriage with a brother of the deceased husband, was introduced. The widow was allowed generally a choice between the brothers, but with the elder lay the right if he chose to exercise it. This form of marriage was known as *chadar dálna*, or throwing the sheet; also as *Karewa* (Karíhúí), signifying a woman who had been married. As the origin of the practice was to secure the succession in the family, the offspring of these unions were considered as legitimate as those of the more formal *shádi* or *vyáh*, and enjoyed the same right to inheritance; but as a matter of precedence and dignity they were not held in equal honour. The convenience of the *chadar dálna* marriage, especially in time of war, when the elaborate ceremonial of the *shádi* was impossible, or unsuited to the rank or caste of the bride, who might be a slave girl or a captive, caused its general extension to other unions than those with the brother's widow. But in these cases, the object of securing the succession not being at issue, the *chadar dálna* wife and her issue were not held of much account, and her place, indeed, was little above that of the ordinary concubine. The informality of the practice rendered it suspicious, and it was notorious that many slave-girls on the death of their masters, supported by the wholesale perjury so generally available in the East, claimed estates on the strength of a pretended *chadar dálna* marriage. This was the case with the mother of Mahárájá Dhulíp Singh, who was acknowledged as successor to the throne of Lahore as the result of a palace intrigue, although his mother was a mere slave-girl.

The right of the widow to re-marry at her own choice, when she was not claimed by her late husband's brother, was everywhere admitted, and there are instances of women making even third marriages, known as *threwa.*

With regard to the succession of sons there were two customs, one known as *chadarband,* confined to the Sikhs of the Mánjha, and the other *bhaiband,* practised by the Málwá Sikhs. The first divided the property among the mothers in equal shares; the second in equal shares among the sons. For example, supposing a man left two widows, one of whom had one son and the other three; by *chadarband* the single son of the first widow would take half the estate and his three half-brothers would each take a sixth. By *bhaiband* the four sons would each receive a quarter.

This irregular practice in marriage is not followed by the higher castes, Bráhmans and Khattrís, who may have embraced Sikhism. They follow the old Hindu ritual, but even then are regarded as outcasts by the orthodox community who will not give them a daughter in marriage except for very large sums of money. In such cases the girl is considered as dead by her own family.

Daughters and their issue were in all cases held incompetent to inherit, as, if this had been allowed in a society in which girls were always married as soon as they reached puberty, estates would have passed out of the possession of the original family.

The practice of *Satí*, or widow-burning, was common in the case of chiefs of high degree, when the women were not allowed to claim their privilege of re-marriage, and it was often extended to the female servants and concubines of the deceased. When Mahárájá Ranjít Singh died one of his wives, Mahtab Devi, was burnt with him [1], and three ladies of his zenána of the rank of Ráni. On the funeral pile of his son, Mahárájá Kharak Singh, one of his *chadar dálna* wives, a beautiful woman named Isar Kour, was burnt. She was unwilling to be a *Satí*; and it is said that she was forced to burn by the minister Rájá Dhyán Singh. Two of the wives of Nao Nihál Singh, the grandson of Ranjít Singh, became *Satís*. The last two widow-burnings in the Punjab were remarkable as showing

[1] This lady was a Rájput, the natural daughter of Rájá Sansar Chand Katoch. The *Sati* was probably a voluntary one, for the proud Rájput women used to consider the disagreeable duty of burning themselves with their husbands a privilege attaching to their blue blood. When the handsome Rájá Suchet Singh, great uncle to the present Mahárájá of Kashmír, was killed at Lahore, his ten wives and the three hundred unmarried ladies of his zenána committed *Sati*, some at Lahore, 150 at Rámnagar, where his head was brought, and the others at Jammu or their own homes.

this curious Hindu custom at its worst and at its best; in other words, where the victims were brutally murdered in the name of religion, or where they voluntarily and cheerfully met the death of fire as the glorious crown of a life of self-sacrifice and devotion.

The first took place on the 22nd of September, 1845, when the body of the debauched and infamous Jowáhir Singh, brother of Ráni Jindan and minister of the State, who had been killed by the infuriated soldiery who rightly suspected him of treachery to the Khálsa, was burnt on the plain outside the Lahore fort. It was decided that his four wives should be burnt with him, though the unfortunate women begged for their lives. The scene at the funeral pile was a shocking one. The troops, who had lost all discipline, stripped the women of their jewels and tore away their nose-rings. A *Satí* is considered a sacred object among Hindus, and her last words prophetic. At the feet of these wretched women, Rájá Dina Náth, who was officially present on behalf of the Ráni, and many others, fell down, imploring their blessings. The *Satís* blessed him and the Mahárájá, but cursed the army of the Khálsa. When asked the fate of the Punjab, they answered that during the year the country would lose its independence, the Khálsa be overthrown, and the wives of the men of the army would be widows. They were then forced into the flames of the funeral pile; but the prophecy came true, and no curse was more amply fulfilled.

The next *Satí* was of the widow of Sirdár Shám

Singh of Attári, one of the noblest and best of the Sikhs. He was killed at Sobráon. He had denounced the war with the English, and well foresaw what its termination must be. But he resolved to fight for the Khálsa, and on the night before Sobráon he swore on the *Granth* never to leave the field defeated. In the morning he dressed himself in white and, having mounted his white mare, addressed his men, begging them, as true sons of the Khálsa, to die rather than yield. During the first part of the battle he was everywhere present, urging the Sikhs to fight bravely; and it was not till he saw that all was lost that he spurred forward against the 50th Regiment, waving his sword and calling on his men to follow him. Some fifty of them obeyed the call, but were driven into the river Sutlej, and Shám Singh fell dead from his horse, pierced with seven bullets. After the battle his servants begged permission to search for his body. The old Sirdár, conspicuous by his white dress and long white beard, was discovered where the dead lay thickest. His servants placed the body on a raft and swam with it across the river; but it was not till the third day that it reached his home at Attári. His widow, who knew his resolution not to survive defeat, had already burnt herself with the clothes which the Sirdár had worn on his wedding day. This was the last *Satí* in the Punjab, and the pillar which marks the spot where it took place is still standing outside the walls of Attári.

Illegitimacy was held to be a bar to succession, but,

as may readily be supposed, in rude times, when the will of the strongest was often the only law, bastards not unfrequently obtained a position to which they were not entitled by birth. Moreover when throwing a sheet over a woman (*chadar dálna*) gave her the full status of a legitimate wife, it was difficult to distinguish between the lawful son and the bastard. There were again degrees in illegitimacy, and well-recognised distinctions between legitimate and illegitimate concubinage, the son of a common slave girl not ranking with one born of a girl of respectable position who may have come to the house of the chief as one of the attendants on his bride.

With regard to the succession of collaterals there was some difference of practice, but the general rule was against it, as indeed is proved by the custom of the *Karewa* marriage under which a man taking the widow of his deceased brother acquired rights of succession which he would not otherwise have possessed. Mahárájá Ranjít Singh altogether refused to allow collaterals any rights, and on failure of male heirs of the body he invariably claimed an estate, though he ordinarily reassigned it to a near relation on payment of a heavy fine or *nazrána*. The practice of the English in the protected Cis-Sutlej States was similar and on much stronger grounds, for the Málwá Sikhs had been far more subordinate to the Delhi Government than those of the Mánjha, who were the conquerors and freeholders of their own lands, while Ranjít Singh was merely the most successful among robber chiefs, *primus inter pares*. The British Government succeeded to many large estates under this rule, such as Búriya, Ambála, Thanesar, Diálgarh, Rudour, Mustafábád, Firozpur, and Kaithal. After 1860 the Government decided to change its policy, and, conferring on all the principal chiefs the privilege of adoption, practically waived for ever its right of escheat. That this policy was, in the main, wise may be admitted, and its results have been to strengthen the position of the Government with the native States. But it may be questioned whether it was not carried out in too general and liberal a manner, and whether it would not have been more judicious to have granted the right of adoption for a term as a special reward for the highest services to the Government, renewable or denied after full consideration of the circumstances of each case. As it is, the indiscriminate grant of the right of adoption by Lord Canning, making the Government an earthly Providence whose favours are conferred alike on the just and the unjust, has deprived it for ever of the power of rewarding loyalty and devotion most splendidly, and of most effectively punishing treason.

CHAPTER IV

The State of the Punjab at Ranjít Singh's Birth

Guru Govind Singh had announced to his disciples that he was the last of the prophets. With his death, the work of forming the Sikhs into a proud, ambitious and warlike people, inspired with deadly hatred of their Mussulman invaders, conquerors and masters, was complete. The Khálsa, fully armed and equipped for victory, had sprung from the brain of the great Guru, as Minerva from the head of Jupiter. But it was only in organization, in martial spirit, and in the sympathy of a common faith and baptism that the elect of the sword were, as yet, strong. They were few in number when opposed to the legions of their enemies; they were poor and of small repute if compared with their oppressors who commanded the whole resources of Hindustán. With nothing but their faith, their brave hearts and their swords, they engaged in a death-struggle with the Mughal Empire which, in the days of the Emperor Aurangzeb, raised a revenue estimated at eighty millions sterling, or double that which is now raised in actual taxation by the British Government from a larger population. Fortunately for the Sikhs they had an ally in the ferocious bigotry of the Emperor which created enemies to his throne in every Feudatory Hindu State, and eventually brought the magnificent fabric of Empire to the ground. Despotisms that have no other foundation than the personal qualities of individuals can never be secure. Sagacity, unselfishness and benevolence are not the fruits which grow on the thorns and brambles of tyranny. Ignorant, debauched, cruel, and fanatical despots are far more likely to turn up when a cynical Fortune deals the cards. Had it been possible to produce a succession of princes like Akbar the magnificent, who, take him all in all, was perhaps the man most brilliant and complete, in his intellectual ascendency, of all historical autocrats, the Mughal Empire might have been flourishing to-day, and English traders would still be humbly soliciting imperial favour at Delhi, before the peacock throne. But the bigoted intolerance of the Emperor Aurangzeb, who, apart from his religion, was of blameless life and possessed of many accomplishments, did more to ruin the Empire than the extravagances of his predecessors and successors.

As to the Sikhs, his persecutions strengthened their obstinate attachment to their faith, and the threat of death and torture never won Islám a single convert. The blood of the martyrs was, as ever, the seed of the Church. Impotent to crush it entirely, Aurangzeb only succeeded in infusing its spirit into fresh votaries, and in inspiring the Sikh people with that hatred of the Muhammadan creed which is still glowing in the embers, ready to burst into fierce life should the British Government ever withdraw its restraining hand. Delhi has seen this spirit revived, so have the Afghans of the North-West; and it will blaze high should the Ghazis of Central Asia madly think of marching again to the plunder of Hindustán.

The history of the Sikhs from the death of Guru Govind Singh to the birth of Ranjít Singh can only be briefly noticed, the more so as I have already given a sketch of the origin and character of the Sikhs and their creed, so that it may be readily understood what were the men whom the great Mahárájá ruled and the nature of the doctrine of which he became the official representative. The material for an historical record of the seventy-two years which this period covers (1708–1780) is meagre and unreliable so far as the Mánjha Sikhs are concerned. More is known of the Southern Sikhs. As to the Muhammadan record, it is full of great and varied interest, and includes the invasions of Nadír Sháh, of Ahmad Sháh, and the gradual decline and disintegration of the Mughal Empire, whose governors and lieutenants threw off the authority of the Emperors and declared themselves independent.

The military successor of Govind Singh was Banda, who during the reign of Aurangzeb's three successors showed great energy and some military talent, defeating the imperial troops on more than one occasion, and ravaging the country of the Bári Doáb until he was, in 1716, captured with some thousands of his followers and carried a prisoner to Delhi. There he was put to death with every refinement of torture after having been compelled to kill his son with his own hands. After this crushing defeat, we hear little of the Sikhs until the invasion of Nadír Sháh, whose easy conquest of Delhi and plunder of the city so weakened the Mughal Government that the Sikhs took heart and again prepared for battle. All Muhammadans, whether Persians, Afgháns, or Mughals, were to them accursed, and with equal alacrity they attacked the scattered detachments of Nadír Sháh's army, or plundered the baggage of Ahmad Sháh Abdáli, who after the assassination of Nadír Sháh had become master of Afghánistán and invaded the Punjab in 1747. The conduct of this prince to the Sikhs was conciliatory, and he would have been glad to enlist them on his side, first against the Delhi Government and then against the Maráthás, whom he defeated in turn. But the Sikhs, although they hated the Mughals, bore no love to the Afgháns, and had no wish to build up at Delhi an empire stronger than that which had preceded it and bind the yoke more firmly on their own necks. The horsemanship, frugal habits, and rapidity of movement of the Sikhs made them formidable opponents, and although they received constant and severe defeats from the better armed and disciplined Muhammadan troops, they never lost heart and only dispersed to reappear shortly afterwards in increasing swarms. Ahmad Sháh, who was a very brilliant leader, though he had little talent for organization or administration and quickly lost the provinces he conquered, invaded India year after year, sometimes marching as far south as Delhi, at other times going no further than Lahore or the Sutlej. On each occasion he had to reckon with the Sikhs, who ever gained greater confidence and power and were forming themselves into confederacies, or *misls*, in which a number of robber chiefs agreed, after a somewhat democratic and equal fashion, to follow the flag and fight under the general orders of one powerful leader. This organization made them more formidable. The several chiefs built their forts in convenient places and gradually overran the whole plain country of the Punjab, shutting up the Muhammadan governors in their forts at Sirhind, Dinánagar, and Lahore, which last city they twice seized and occupied for some time. They rebuilt the sacred places of Amritsar and refilled the Tank of the Water of Immortality. When the Afghán prince came down, year after year, from the mountains, the Sikhs retired from before him; as he retired they again seized the prey they had temporarily abandoned. The years 1761-62 were the turning-point in Sikh history, and as such require brief notice, for they contain the first stand of the Khálsa against a regular army. Its defeat, although severe, gave it so much confidence that it was able, the following year, to conquer the province of Sirhind, and to found on a secure basis the great chiefships of the Cis-Sutlej.

Zín Khán had been appointed by Ahmad Sháh, in 1761, as his governor at Sirhind. But no sooner had the Afghán turned his face homeward than the Sikhs, collecting in great numbers, besieged Zín Khán in his fort and would certainly have taken it and annihilated the garrison had not help come in the form of the Mussulman Khán of Maler Kotla. When Ahmad Sháh returned, the following year, to India, he resolved to punish the Sikhs for their insolent attack on Sirhind. They had assembled near Barnála, then the principal town in Patiála territory, and, in addition to the chiefs of the Cis-Sutlej, there were many of the leaders of the Mánjha Sikhs who had crossed the Sutlej as Ahmad Sháh advanced. The movements of the Afgháns had been so rapid that the Sikhs were surprised, surrounded and compelled to give battle, and were defeated with the loss of 20,000 men and many prisoners, among whom was Ala Singh the chief of Patiála, for whose ransom five lakhs of rupees were demanded. This sum was paid with great difficulty, and Ahmad Sháh, who was a man of great sagacity, thinking it would be wise to conciliate the Sikhs after having given them so convincing a proof of his power, embraced Ala Singh and bestowed on him a dress of honour with the title of Rájá.

This unwonted dignity aroused against Ala Singh

the jealousy and anger of all the other chiefs, who declared that he had betrayed them, that the title was the price of his treachery, and that it was disgraceful for a Sikh to accept an honour conferred by a Muhammadan, a foreigner and an enemy. They would have avenged upon him their defeat had not Sirdár Jassa Singh Ahluwalia, at that time far more influential than Ala Singh himself, taken his part. Matters were, at length, smoothed over, but it was necessary for Alá Singh to prove by his actions that he was not a servant of the Duráni king.

No sooner had Ahmad Sháh returned to Kábul than the Sikhs regained courage. The confederacies, north and south of the Sutlej, for once laid aside their feuds and jealousies and united for another great effort against Sirhind. Ala Singh joined with ardour in the expedition. The Sikhs from the Mánjha assembled in numbers in the neighbourhood of Sirhind, after having captured the town and fort of Kasúr below Lahore; and the chiefs of the Málwá joined them, till the army, almost entirely cavalry, numbered 23,000 men. Zín Khán, the governor, trusting to that dread of regular troops which the Sikhs had ever shown, came beyond the town to give them battle, but he was killed and his force utterly routed. The Sikhs immediately took possession of the town, which they sacked and destroyed in revenge for the murder of the children of their prophet, and the province of Sirhind was divided among the conquerors, the town and the district surrounding it being allotted to Rájá Ala Singh. Ahmad Sháh, who returned the following year, made no attempt to recover Sirhind or appoint another governor, but accepting the logic of events assigned the district to Ala Singh on payment of an annual tribute[1].

Thus the Sikhs, both by their defeat and their victory, acquired a status which they did not before possess, and had they known how to put aside private jealousies and unite habitually as they had done for the conquest of Sirhind, they would have become as formidable and irresistible in North India as the Maráthás in the South and West. But the democratic nature of the Sikh faith, responding to the natural sentiment of the people, resisted all attempts at dictation by one central authority, until Mahárájá Ranjít Singh broke down opposition and reduced rivals and enemies to a common obedience.

The history of Sikh development between this year 1762 and the birth of Ranjít Singh in 1780, or rather to the death of his father Mahán Singh and his own succession to the headship of the Sukarchakia *misl* in 1791, a period of great importance and interest, must be studied elsewhere[2]. All that

[1] *The Rájás of the Punjab.*

[2] The only works in which the history of this period has been treated in detail are my *Punjab Chiefs* and *Rájás of the Punjab.* In the first the full account of the various *misls* north of the Sutlej will be found under such heads as the Rámgarhias, the Bhangis, the Kanheyas; while the second is the history of the Phúlkian and Ahluwalia *misls.*

is necessary here is to explain the general Sikh organization in *misls* or confederacies and the districts which were held by the several chiefs.

The Sikh *misls* were, in popular estimation, twelve in number, and although this enumeration is misleading, and several of the included confederacies were hardly of sufficient importance to warrant their being placed in the list, yet it may for convenience be here adhered to. I will, however, place them in what I consider the order of their importance at the time of the birth of Mahárájá Ranjít Singh.

1. Phúlkian.	7. Krora Singhia.
2. Ahluwalia.	8. Nishánia.
3. Bhangi.	9. Sukarchakia.
4. Kanheya.	10. Dulelwala.
5. Rámgarhia.	11. Nakkais.
6. Singhpúria.	12. Shahíds.

Of these, Nos. 2, 3, 4, 5, 9 and 11, held lands north of the Sutlej, and the remaining six, south of that river. The Phúlkian *misl* was composed of a group of chiefs descended from a common ancestor, and represented at the present day by their descendants, the Mahárájá of Patiála, the Rájás of Jínd and Nábha, the Sirdárs of Bhadour, Malod and many others of less importance. It played a very important part in early Sikh history, but in spite of the family connection of its members or perhaps in consequence of it, united action by the *misl* was rare and its power was not equal to its opportunities.

The Ahluwalia family was founded by Sádho Singh,

a Ját of the Kalál or distiller caste, who settled the village of Ahlu from which the family took its name. But the true founder of the confederacy was Sirdár Jassa Singh, fifth in the descent from Sádho, who was born in 1718, ten years after the death of Guru Govind Singh. He rose to distinction and was a man of great ability and a successful military leader. He did more than almost any chief to consolidate the Sikh power, and at the time of his death, in 1783, was probably the most influential of the Sikh chiefs. His possessions were chiefly in the tract of country between the rivers Sutlej and Beas.

The Bhangis took their name from the enslavement to *bhang*, an intoxicating preparation of hemp, of their famous leader Sirdár Harí Singh, who, with his brothers Jhanda Singh and Ganda Singh, made his head-quarters in the Amritsar district and overran the neighbouring country and captured and held the city of Múltán for several years. They were crushed by Mahárájá Ranjít early in his career, as will hereafter be told.

The Kanheyas were quite as powerful as the Bhangis and retained their possessions longer owing to their connection by marriage with the Mahárájá, Ranjít Singh. Their chief, Jai Singh, married his infant grand-daughter Mahtab Kour, in 1786, to Ranjít Singh, who was himself only six years old. When Jai Singh died, in 1789, his daughter-in-law Sada Kour, the mother of Mahtab Kour, a widow of great ability and unscrupulousness, took command of the confederacy, and held her own against her son-in-law, successfully, till 1820. The possessions of the Kanheyas included a large part of the Amritsar and Gurdáspur districts. A second lady of this house, Ráni Chand Kour, who married Prince Kharak Singh, the only son of the great Mahárájá, had as stormy and eventful a life as Sada Kour, and the adventures of these intriguing women show how powerful female influence was among the Sikhs under the liberal creed of Nának and Govind Singh.

The Rámgarhia *misl* shared with the Kanheyas the sacred city of Amritsar and the neighbouring districts. It could at the height of its power put eight thousand fighting men into the field. Sirdár Jassa Singh, who was the most distinguished of its captains, succeeded to its leadership in 1758. He first fortified Amritsar, a portion of which he surrounded with a high mud wall, calling it Rám Rowni or the fort of God. It was soon attacked and destroyed by Adina Beg, the imperial governor of the Jálandhar Doáb; but, on his death, Jassa Singh rebuilt it, and renamed it Rámgarh, from which the confederacy took its name.

He was a famous fighting baron and made long expeditions, plundering up to the walls of Delhi. On one occasion he penetrated into the heart of the city and carried off four guns from the Mughal quarter. The governor of Meerut paid him tribute.

The Singhpúria confederacy was at one time very powerful, and, before the days of Jassa Singh Ahluwalia and Ala Singh of Patiála, its founder, Sirdár

Kapúr Singh was perhaps the most renowned of the Sikh barons. He was known as Nawáb, one of the few instances of a Sikh taking a distinctively Muhammadan title. He seized the village and district of Faizullapúr near Amritsar from Faizullá Khán, and gave it the name of Singhpúra, whence the title of the *misl*, though it is as often known as Faizullapúra. This chief died in 1753, and Jassa Singh Ahluwalia succeeded to the greater part of his influence, though his nephew Khushhál Singh and his descendants kept possession of the territory. This confederacy held portions of Ludhiána, Núrpur, Jálandhar, and the north-western portion of the Ambála district.

The Krora Singhias, who took their name from Sirdár Krora Singh, had possessions chiefly between the Jumna and Makanda rivers. The powerful family of Kalsia was the principal member of the *misl*, and is still a ruling house in the Cis-Sutlej: also Sirdár Baghel Singh of Chiloundi, whose family is now extinct.

The Nishánias, who took their name from the *Nishán* or banner of the Khálsa, were never of much consequence. Sirdár Jai Singh, the most important of the confederacy, obtained his estates after the conquest of Sirhind in 1763. Members of the *misl* held Ambála, Liddrán, Shábábád, Amloh, and other districts.

The Sukarchakias are famous not from the amount of their original possessions but from the fact that Ranjít Singh was their last representative, and their history will be included in that of the Mahárájá.

The Dulolwala confederacy took its name from the village of Sirdár Tára Singh, who was its principal leader, and who, with his followers, held a great portion of the upper Jálandhar Doáb and the northern portions of Ambála and Ludhiána, with some estates in Firozpur. The Nakkais inhabited what is known as the Nakka country lying between Lahore and Gogaira in the direction of Múltán. It was never a powerful confederacy, but could bring into the field some two thousand horsemen with camel-swivels and a few guns. But the Játs of this part of the Punjab are notoriously brave, and under Sirdár Hira Singh and Rám Singh they acquired territory worth nine lakhs of rupees per annum, in Gogaira, Kasúr, and Sharakpur.

The Shahíds, the last of the confederacies, were rather a religious than a military body, though the priests fought in those days as well as the laymen. The Khálsa was the true embodiment of the church militant. The founder of the Shahíd *misl* was Sudda Singh, the *muhant* or head of the shrine at Talwandi, where Guru Govind Singh had made his resting-place (Damdama). He was killed fighting against the Muhammadan governor of Jálandhar, and his head having been struck off he is reported to have ridden some distance and killed several of the enemy before he fell from his horse. Hence he was known as the martyr (shahíd), and his followers took his name. This confederacy, which used to join itself to others rather than fight on its own account, obtained estates about Ránia, Khari and Jaroli, and its representatives still hold charge of the sacred shrine of Damdama.

Such is a sketch of the fighting confederacies of the Sikhs during the eighteenth century and the first part of the nineteenth. But their composition was always changing, and their possessions passed from one hand to another very rapidly. They fought against each other more often than against the common enemy the Muhammadans, and their internecine war was only ended by Mahárájá Ranjít Singh crushing all who were not shielded by the British guarantee. Even within the borders of each confederacy itself, the barons were always quarrelling, and first one chief and then another took the lead. This was due to the constitution of Sikhism, under which no such thing as vassalage or feudal superiority was acknowledged. The principle of the creed was fraternity, and the Sikhs boasted of being communities of independent soldiers. While the Khálsa was still young and enthusiastic, and the power of no individual chief was inordinately great, this idea of independence represented a state of things not far removed from the truth; but as the more important chiefships gradually increased in power, their smaller neighbours were compelled, either for protection against others or to avoid absorption altogether, to place themselves under the protection of some leader able to defend them, rendering in return service in the field.

All that a Sikh chief asked in these days from a follower was a horse and a matchlock. All that a follower sought was protection and permission to plunder in the name of God and the Guru under the banner of the chief. There was little question of pay All Sikhs were theoretically equal, and he who, like Amar Singh Majíthia, could pierce a tree through with an arrow, or like Harí Singh Nalwa, could kill a tiger with a blow of his sword, might soon ride with followers behind him and call himself a Sirdár. The time came when, like the Jews, the Sikhs took a king, and in some degree forgot the dream of equality which had been so dear to them.

But all the great families, north and south of the Sutlej, have the same origin: the law of force, the keen sword and the strong hand were the foundations upon which Sikh society, as indeed every other powerful society in the world, was founded. To attract followers by his power and success was the main desire of every Sikh chief. Who they were, and what were their antecedents, were matters of no consequence if only they could fight and ride, which almost every Sikh could do. In these days every village became a fort, built on a high mound to overlook the plain country, with but one entrance, and narrow lanes in which two men could hardly walk abreast. A neighbour, as with the Jews and Samaritans, was synonymous with an enemy, and husbandmen ploughed the fields with matchlocks by their side. No man could consider his land, his horse, or his wife secure unless he was strong enough to defend them; for although the Sikh leaders were best pleased with the spoil of Muhammadans or the capture of an imperial convoy, they were more robbers than patriots and plundered with frank impartiality. One thing in their favour must be said, which raises them far above the Pindáris of Central India or the dacoits of Bengal: they fought and plundered like men and not like demons. There are few stories in Sikh history of outrage to women and torture to men such as stain the pages of South Indian history with cruelty and blood. Many a pretty Játní girl was, it is true, carried off in a foray, but she was generally a willing captive. She had been taught to consider courage and strength the only qualities to desire in a husband, and was quite ready to yield herself a prize to the man who had won her in fair fight, and who would make her his lawful wife, though he had killed her brothers and burned their village. Yet, while the Sikhs were undoubted robbers, and though cattle-lifting was the one honourable profession amongst them, as on the Scottish border a few hundred years ago, their enthusiasm for their faith, their hatred to the Muhammadans who had so long trampled them under foot, who had killed their prophets and thrown down their altars, gave them a certain dignity, and to their objects and expeditions an almost national interest.

The Sikh army was known as the *Dal Khálsa*, the army of God, sometimes the *Budha Dal* or veteran army. It consisted for the most part of cavalry called *Kattiawand*, who found their own horses and received a double share of prize money. Each chief, in proportion to his means, furnished horses and arms to his retainers who were called Bárgirs; and as the first tribute exacted from a conquered district was horses, the infantry soldier was, after a successful campaign, generally transformed into a trooper. The infantry were considered an inferior branch of the service, and were only used for garrison and sentry duty, and the battles of the Sikhs were invariably cavalry actions. The only infantry who enjoyed any respect were the Akális. These were a fanatical body of devotees, who dressed in dark blue and wore round their turbans steel quoits, partly for show and partly as weapons, though they were not very effective.

Their other distinctive signs were a knife stuck in the turban, a sword slung round their neck, and a wooden club. These men, excited by hemp, were generally the first to storm a town, and often did excellent service; but they were lawless and uncertain, and, in peaceful times, enjoyed almost boundless license. The Sikh weapon was the sword, with which the cavalry were very skilful. Bows and arrows were used by the infantry, and a few matchlocks; but powder was scarce and its use little liked by the Sikhs, who were never at ease with a musket in their hands. For the same reasons they possessed scarcely any artillery; and although Ranjít Singh, with the aid of French and Italian officers, formed a very powerful and well-appointed artillery, it was, to the last, a branch of the service hated by every true Sikh, and principally filled by Muhammadans. The prize money taken in a campaign was equally shared among the combatants: if a soldier was wounded he invariably received compensation, and if he was killed, his son or nearest male relative was entertained in his place.

The chiefs or barons were known by some cognomen which specially distinguished them; for the Hindu names were few in number and the suffix *Singh* was universal. Generally this addition was taken from their birthplace, or from a town they had conquered, as Jassa Singh, Ahluwalia; sometimes from a personal peculiarity or attribute, good or bad. As examples of these may be quoted Nidhán Singh, Panjhathah (the five-handed, from his great prowess in battle); Lehna Singh, Chimni (from his short stature); Mohr Singh, Lamba (the tall); Sher Singh, Kamla (the fool); Karm Singh, Nírmala (the spotless), and a hundred more with which Sikh history is full; and of which many have descended to the present day as an honoured part of the family name.

CHAPTER V

The Mahárájá

No traveller can have visited the Punjab without becoming familiar with the features of the great Mahárájá. Although half a century has passed since his death, his name is still a household word in the province; his portrait is still preserved in castle and in cottage. It is a favourite subject with the ivory painters of Amritsar and Delhi, by whom the Mahárájá is ordinarily represented in middle or old age, and it is rare to find one of him in youth or in the prime of life. The fine arts were not much patronized in early days at the Court of Lahore. Late in life Ranjít Singh did not make a pleasing picture, though his appearance was striking and memorable. Hard work, the exposure of numerous campaigns, drunkenness and debauchery aged him before his time, and left him at fifty a worn-out, broken-down, old man.

There are many contemporary descriptions of him. This by Baron Hügel is as vivid as any:—

'In person he is short and mean-looking, and had he not distinguished himself by his great talents he would be passed by without being thought worthy of observation. Without exaggeration I must call him the most ugly and unprepossessing man I saw throughout the Punjab. His left eye, which is quite closed, disfigures him less than the other, which is always rolling about wide open and is much distorted by disease. The scars of the small-pox on his face do not run into one another but form so many dark pits in his greyish-brown skin; his short straight nose is swollen at the tip; the skinny lips are stretched tight over his teeth which are still good; his grizzled beard, very thin on the cheeks and upper lip, meets under the chin in matted confusion, and his head, which is sunk very much on his broad shoulders, is too large for his height, and does not seem to move easily. He has a thick muscular neck, thin arms and legs, the left foot and left arm drooping, and small well-formed hands. He will sometimes hold a stranger's hand fast within his own for half-an-hour, and the nervous irritation of his mind is shown by the continual pressure on one's fingers. His costume always contributes to increase his ugliness, being in winter the colour of gamboge from the Pagri (the turban or Sikh cloth) down to his very socks and slippers. When he seats himself in a common English chair with his feet drawn under him, the position is one particularly unfavourable to him, but as soon as he mounts his horse and with his black shield at his back puts him on his mettle, his whole form seems animated by the spirit within, and assumes a certain grace of which nobody could believe it susceptible. In spite of the paralysis affecting one side, he manages his horse with the utmost ease.'

This striking picture is unprepossessing enough; but, previous to his paralytic seizure which occurred in 1834, Ranjít Singh, although short of stature and disfigured by that cruel disease which was wont to decimate the Punjab, and which still, in spite of vaccination, claims numerous victims, was the *beau idéal* of a soldier, strong, spare, active, courageous, and enduring. An excellent horseman, he would remain the whole day in the saddle without showing any sign of fatigue. His love for horses amounted to a passion, and he maintained an enormous stud for his personal use collected from every part of India, Arabia, and Persia. He was also a keen sportsman and an accomplished swordsman. At Rúpar, in 1831, he competed with success with his own troopers and those of Skinner's Horse in tent-pegging and feats of swordsmanship. His dress was scrupulously simple. In winter and spring he wore generally a warm dress of saffron-coloured Kashmír cloth; in the hot weather white muslin without jewel or ornament, except on occasions of special display or state. This simplicity in the matter of personal adornment may often be observed in native princes or statesmen of intellectual eminence. Like Europeans, they despise the decorations of savages and women. The late Mahárájá Túkají Ráo Holkar of Indore, Rájá Sir Dinkar Ráo, and Sir Sálár Jang the great minister of the Nizám, habitually dressed as plainly as the humblest of their employés. But Ranjít Singh did not require jewels to make him conspicuous. It was strange indeed to observe how complete was his ascendency, even when he had become feeble, blind, and paralysed, over his brilliant court of fierce and turbulent chiefs. Fakír Azizuddin, who had been sent on a mission to Lord William

Bentinck at Simla in 1831, was asked by an English officer of which eye the Mahárájá was blind. His answer well illustrated the attitude of his Court towards him. 'The splendour of his face is such,' said the Fakír, 'that I have never been able to look close enough to discover.'

The Mahárájá was endowed with some of the most conspicuous and undoubted signs and characteristics of greatness. Judged from a commonplace, ethical standpoint, and measured by a conventional rule, he had no moral character at all. He had a large and indeed an unusual share of the weaknesses and vices which grow up, like ill weeds, in human nature, and his moral being seemed, at a superficial glance, as dwarfed and distorted as its physical envelope. He was selfish, false and avaricious; grossly superstitious, shamelessly and openly drunken and debauched. In the respectable virtues he had no part; but in their default he was still great. With him, as with the most illustrious leaders of men, from Cæsar and Alexander to Napoleon, intellectual strength was not allied to moral rectitude. He was great because he possessed in an extraordinary degree the qualities without which the highest success cannot be attained; and the absence of the commonplace virtues which belong to the average citizen neither diminished nor affected in any way the distinction of his character. He was a born ruler, with the natural genius of command. Men obeyed him by instinct and because they had no power to disobey. The control which he exercised, even in the closing years of his life, over the whole Sikh people, nobles, priests and people, was the measure of his greatness.

To the highest courage he added a perseverance which no obstacles could exhaust, and he did not fail in his undertakings because he never admitted the possibility of failure. His political sagacity was great, and was shown in nothing more convincingly than in his determined friendship with the English, when he had once realized that they were safe friends and very dangerous enemies. In spite of strong temptations, and although they had rudely opposed his most cherished ambition of conquering the Cis-Sutlej provinces, he firmly held to the English alliance throughout his reign; and the tradition of this friendship remained so strong after his death that it kept the weak and drunken Mahárájá Sher Singh faithful, when the Punjab was in a tumult and a British army had been destroyed in Afghánistán. He possessed the faculty which is one of the highest attributes of genius, and for lack of which many brilliantly gifted men have suffered shipwreck—the faculty of choosing his subordinates well and wisely. He knew men, and he selected each servant for the special work which he could best perform, and consequently he was, even in a corrupt and violent age, wonderfully well served. His natural avarice and rapacity were tempered by his appreciation of the advantages of generosity in rewarding good service, and he gave liberally of what he had plundered from other people.

His favourites were granted large estates or assignments of revenue, and this was the more necessary as they were expected to spend the greater part of their income in the entertainment and maintenance of armed retainers to be ready at the instant call of their chief. Everything that Ranjit Singh possessed had been ruthlessly taken from someone else; and lavishness is the first cousin of avarice and greed, as may be seen every day at Monte Carlo or wherever gamblers most assemble.

Although it would be to violate the truth of history to conceal or disguise the many faults and vices of Ranjít Singh, yet it would be trivial to judge him or them without full consideration of the manners of the society in which he lived. Every age and people have their own standard of virtue; and what is to-day held to be atrocious or disreputable may, one hundred years hence, be the fashion. The vices of civilization are not purer than those of barbarism; they are only more decently concealed when it is considered worth while to practise the hypocrisy which is declared to be the tribute which vice pays to virtue. In the days of the Georges, our ancestors drank as heavily and ostentatiously as any of the Sirdárs of the Lahore Court. 'Drunk as a lord' was a popular saying which very fairly expressed the habits of the aristocracy in England in the eighteenth century. To-day the fashion has changed and men drink less or more secretly. In the matter of the relations between the sexes the morality of the Punjab was exceedingly low. Yet the Sikhs had the excuse that the position of women was a degraded one, and as education and sentiment had never placed her, as in Western Europe, upon an elevated pedestal, there was no reason to expect from her or from men any lofty ideas of purity. But if we accept contemporary literature as sufficient evidence, the society of Paris to-day is fully as corrupt as that of the Punjab in 1830; and the bazaars of Lahore, while Ranjít Singh was celebrating the festival of the Holi, were not more shameless than Piccadilly at night in 1892.

So with the political methods of Ranjít Singh. Violence, fraud and rapacity were the very breath of the nostrils of every Sikh chief. They were the arms and the defence of men who in a demoralized and disintegrated society, had to be ready to resist attack and protect their lives and property. It would be as reasonable to reproach the lion for the use of his teeth and claws, as to regard the force or fraud which made up the military and political history of the Mahárájá and the chiefs of his Court as more than the ordinary and necessary result of their life and surroundings. To-day, the ruler of Afghánistán conducts his administration on principles very similar to those of Ranjít Singh, yet the British Government, with whom he is in subordinate and feudatory alliance, does not offer a remonstrance, because it understands that savage races require drastic treatment, and that where one people can be governed by syllogisms, another only understands the argument of the headsman's sword and the gallows. These considerations must have full and emphatic weight allowed to them when estimating the character of Mahárájá Ranjit Singh.

We only succeed in establishing him as a hero, as a ruler of men and as worthy of a pedestal in that innermost shrine where history honours the few human beings to whom may be indisputably assigned the palm of greatness, if we free our minds of prejudice and, discounting conventional virtue, only regard those rare qualities which raise a man supreme above his fellows. Then we shall at once allow that, although sharing in full measure the commonplace and coarse vices of his time and education, he yet ruled the country which his military genius had conquered with a vigour of will and an ability which placed him in the front rank of the statesmen of the century.

The key-note to the Mahárájá's character was selfishness, and it cannot be said that there were any of his servants whom he regarded with gratitude or affection. If there was any exception it was Jamadár Khushhál Singh, a man of inferior ability and degraded habits. But he was served with a devotion which he did not deserve. Sirdár Fateh Singh of Kapúrthala, for whom he publicly made a theatrical demonstration of affection, exchanging turbans in sign of perpetual brotherhood, and who had fought by his side in the campaigns of twenty years, he endeavoured to despoil of his possessions. Sirdár Harí Singh Nalwa, the Murat of the Khálsa and the most dashing of his generals, had no sooner fallen in battle with the Afgháns in his service, than he seized all his large estates and left his four sons to comparative poverty. He did not approve of hereditary wealth and honour, and, like Tarquinius Superbus, struck down all the tall poppies in his garden. Sirdár Fateh Singh Kálianwala was one of the most powerful Sikh leaders in the early years of the century. At Wazírábád on one occasion, Ranjít Singh asked him to draw his forces on one side that he might see their numbers. To his disgust the greater part of the troops present followed the banner of Fateh Singh. This was enough for the jealous spirit of the Mahárájá who soon afterwards, in 1807, was besieging the fort of Náráyangarh in company with Fateh Singh, as chief in immediate command. After an ineffectual siege of a fortnight, the Mahárájá reproached the Sirdár for his apathy, saying that he preferred remaining at his side to leading the troops in the field. Fateh Singh, angry at the undeserved sarcasm, at once assaulted the fort by a breach which proved impracticable, and was repulsed and slain. The Mahárájá had got rid of his rival, and made over all his estates to another chief.

The Rámgarhia *misl* was one of the most powerful of the Sikh confederacies, and when Ranjít Singh determined to break it up, he feigned a warm affection for its leader Sirdár Jodh Singh. He had a contract of friendship between himself and the Rámgarhia family drawn up, and in the temple of Amritsar, before the Sikh Scriptures, he stamped the paper, in his royal and illiterate way, with his open palm dyed with saffron. For some years he allowed the contract to have effect, for Jodh Singh had become a devoted adherent and his forces were useful in many a campaign. But, in 1816, when the Sirdár died, the opportunity of the Mahárájá came. Having summoned the heirs to meet him at Nadaun to arrange for the succession, he surrounded the reception tent with troops, took them prisoners, and then marched a strong force against Amritsar and seized all the Rámgarhia estates.

With another Jodh Singh, a famous fighting-man, chief of Wazírábád, he acted in a somewhat similar manner. The Mahárájá, thinking him too powerful to attack, invited him to Lahore on a friendly visit. Suspecting Ranjít Singh's intentions, he brought a large force with him which he was asked to send back, a request with which he was too proud to refuse compliance. He attended the Darbár the next day with only twenty-five followers, whom he left outside. He was received by the Mahárájá with the utmost cordiality, but suddenly, Ranjít Singh, rising, made a sign to his people to seize the Sirdár. He, drawing his sword, called on them to come on as he would not be taken alive and had never learned to turn his back on an enemy. His courage so impressed the Mahárájá that he dismissed the chief with honour, rich presents, and an addition to his estates. So far the story is as creditable to Ranjít Singh as to the Sirdár; but when, shortly afterwards, Jodh Singh died, leaving only infant sons, the Mahárájá seized all his possessions; and although he promised to restore Wazírábád when the eldest son should have reached his majority, he never kept, and probably never intended to keep, the promise.

It was not well for a chief to make too ostentatious a display of his wealth. When the young chief of Batálah married his sister to Sirdár Sher Singh, the families spent two lakhs of rupees on the festivities, the like of which had never before been seen in the Gujránwála district. But when the Mahárájá heard of it, and of the boasts of the girl's mother that she had two parolahs[1] of rupees, he at once sent and said that a family which could spend so much on a marriage must be able to afford him a contribution of Rs. 50,000.

With all his rapacity Ranjít Singh was not cruel or bloodthirsty. After a victory or the capture of a fortress he treated the vanquished with leniency and kindness, however stout their resistance might have been, and there were at his Court many chiefs despoiled of their estates but to whom he had given suitable employ, and who accepted their position with the resignation born of Eastern fatalism, which takes the sharpest

[1] Parolah, a Punjábi word for a large basket of clay and wicker-work used for storing grain.

sting out of defeat. The Sirdárs who had been the leaders of the several confederacies which he overthrew, were all in this fashion reduced from equality and rivalship to honourable subjection; and, in addition, there was a large group of Muhammadan Khâns and nobles who would have received short shrift from Govind Singh, but whom Ranjít Singh wisely attached to his fortunes, thereby materially strengthening his position in the western districts. The heads of the Mussulman tribes of Siáls, Ghebas, Tiwánas and Kharrals, and the family of Nawáb Muzaffar Khán of Múltán were included in this group.

The manner in which the Mahárájá became possessed of the Koh-i-Núr, the most famous diamond in the world, and the mare Láili belonging to the Afghán governor of Pesháwar, an animal as famous in her time as the Koh-i-Núr itself, are excellent examples of the character of the Mahárájá for unscrupulousness and pertinacity, and find their place more appropriately in this chapter than in one more purely historical.

The Koh-i-Núr is too well known for description. Supposed to have been worn by the Pándus of Hindu mythology it emerges into the light of history in the sixteenth century with the Emperors Sháh Jahán and Aurangzeb, of whose throne it was the chief ornament. The next owner was that prince of robbers, Nádir Sháh, who obtained it when he plundered Delhi. On his murder it became the prize of Ahmad Sháh Abdáli, and at last, in 1813, when Mahárájá Ranjít

Singh found an opportunity of seizing the diamond, it was in possession of Sháh Shujá, the ex-monarch of Kábul, who had been ousted by his brother, and who came to the Punjab as an exile. Ranjít Singh, partly for political reasons, desiring to have in his hand a weapon which he could use against the Afghán usurper, but chiefly in order to obtain the celebrated jewel, offered Sháh Shujá an asylum at Lahore. The Sikh chroniclers of Ranjít Singh have asserted that Sháh Begam, the wife of Sháh Shujá, sent a messenger to the Maháráj́á, promising him the Koh-i-Núr, if he would protect her husband and not surrender him to Fateh Khán, the governor of Pesháwar, his deadly enemy; that the Maháráj́á at once accepted the present, and sent his trusted general, Mokham Chand, to escort the exiled monarch with all honour to Lahore.

The story told by Sháh Shujá differs from this, and states that the subject of the Koh-i-Núr was never mentioned until Ranjít Singh had him safely in Lahore in the house assigned him for a residence, when he sent brusquely to demand it. The poor fugitive denied having the stone with him; Ranjít Singh sent back and offered a large estate in exchange. Sháh Shujá again asserted that it had been placed for security in the hands of a shráf or money-lender, but that it would become available when the friendship between the Maháráj́á and himself had taken a definite shape and was secured by sufficient guarantees. Ranjít Singh lost his temper, and forgetting the Oriental duty of hospitality, placed a guard of soldiers round the Afghán's house and searched anyone who left it, allowing no food to be sent in. Forged letters were produced which it was stated had been intercepted from Sháh Shujá to his friends in Afghánistán, calling upon them to invade the Punjab and liberate him.

The Sháh was threatened with imprisonment in the fortress of Govindgarh, and at length, after two months' resistance, wearied out with perpetual harassing, seeing his family and servants half-starving and appreciating that longer refusal would only end in his captivity or death, he promised to give up the diamond if the Mahárájá, on his part, would promise him protection and friendship in the most solemn manner. This the Mahárájá did, having a document drawn up in which he promised on the *Ádi Granth* and the *Granth* of the 10th Reign, to be ever the friend of Sháh Shujá and to endeavour to restore him to the throne of Kábul. The Afghán then invited Ranjít Singh to come and receive the diamond in person. He arrived with a few attendants and was received in silence which was unbroken for an hour, when the Mahárájá reminded his new friend and prisoner of the object of his visit. The Sháh ordered one of his servants to bring the diamond. A packet was brought in and unwrapped, and when the Mahárájá saw that it was really the stone he coveted he seized it and left the house without even bidding farewell to the prince. Nor was this all; for, some time afterwards, hearing that his visitors were still the possessors of some magnificent jewels, he sent Bhai Rám Singh with one of his wives to search the house and even the zenána of Sháh Shujá and bring all the valuables that were found. This was done, and it is said that the lady even searched the persons of the wives and female attendants of the Sháh, and everything worth carrying away was kept by the Mahárájá.

The Koh-i-Núr remained at Lahore till 1849, when on the annexation of the Punjab it was surrendered as a token of submission to the Queen of England. To her, as the representative and successor of the Emperors of Delhi, it legitimately descended, quite apart from the right of conquest, on the termination of a war forced on the English by the Sikh army.

The story of the famous mare Láili can be briefly told. She was renowned for her beauty throughout Afghánistán and the Punjab, and Ranjít Singh, in 1826, sent to her owner, Sirdár Yár Muhammad Khán, governor of Pesháwar, to demand her surrender which was refused. Straightway Sirdár Budh Singh Sindhanwalia, one of the best of the Sikh generals, was sent to take possession of the mare, and at the same time to attack Khalifa Syad Ahmad, who was preaching a jihád or holy war against the Sikhs in the Pesháwar hills. He defeated the enemy, with great loss on both sides, but when he reached Pesháwar was informed that Láili had died. On his return to Lahore it was ascertained that this story was false, and another force, under the nominal command of Prince Kharak Singh, was despatched to Pesháwar with orders to buy the mare, or seize her, and if Yár Muhammad would not part with her to depose him from the governorship. The Prince marched to Pesháwar, and Yár Muhammad, who considered that his honour was involved in not surrendering the mare, fled to the hills. Prince Kharak Singh, after holding Pesháwar for eight months, retired, leaving Sirdár Sultán Muhammad Khán as governor; but the Sikh army had not proceeded further than Attock when Yár Muhammad returned and drove out the new governor. General Ventura, who had been left in command of the Sikh army at Attock, was now directed by the Mahárájá to try his hand at the business of the acquisition of the horse, for which he was to offer any price which would be accepted, but, if refused, was to renew hostilities. While Yár Muhammad was hesitating as to his reply, Khalifa Syad Ahmad again descended from the hills and ravaged the villages north of Peshâwar, and the governor, who attempted to drive him back, was killed in the fight which ensued. Láili however had not been surrendered, and General Ventura, after having defeated Syad Ahmad, encamped before Peshâwar and demanded the animal from Sultán Muhammad Khán, whom he promised to confirm in the governorship if he gave her up. But Sultán Muhammad tried as many subterfuges as his brother, and it was not till Ventura had arrested him in his own palace and threatened to hold him a prisoner till Láili was given up, that persistence obtained its deserved success, and the General, becoming the happy possessor of the coveted mare, took her to Lahore where she was received with much rejoicing by the Mahárájá.

Whether the real horse was given up is still doubtful, for there are few created beings that an Afghán cannot or would not deceive. Certainly, at Rúpar in 1831, when the Mahárájá visited the Governor-General, a brown horse was shown as Láili. When Hügel visited Lahore he especially begged to be allowed to see the famous horse, which the Mahárájá told him had cost him sixty lakhs of rupees and twelve thousand men. He describes Láili as magnificently caparisoned, with gold bangles round his legs, a dark grey, with black points, thirteen years old and fully sixteen hands high. This was the horse Ventura assured Hügel that he had obtained with so much difficulty at Peshávar; but, on the other hand, Sikh records always speak of Láili as having been a mare which the name would seem to confirm. So the sex of the true Láili must remain a historical puzzle. Certain it is, that no horse, since that which caused the fall of Troy, has ever been the source of so much trouble and the death of so many brave men.

The Mahárájá was a very hard drinker, and it was his indulgence in frequent and fiery potations which killed him, as it has killed a large number of Indian princes in whose States there is no public opinion sufficiently strong to restrain them from habitual intemperance.

It has been asserted by some of those who are fond of depreciating their own countrymen that intemperance in India is a vice due to foreign importation, and that the Hindus, before the conquest of the country by England, were a perfectly sober people. This was not the case in the Punjab or among the Sikhs. They were always a hard-drinking race. Take the time with which the last chapter is concerned, when the name of the English was unknown to the Sikhs. Rájá Amar Singh of Patiála died of intemperance in 1781, as had his father Sardul Singh in 1753, and his younger brother Lál Singh. Almost every great family had the same record. The sword and the bottle were equally destructive to the barons of the Khálsa.

The favourite liquor of the Mahárájá Ranjít was a fierce compound distilled from corn-brandy, mixed with the juice of meat, opium, musk and various herbs. Of this he drank large quantities in the evening and at night. Most of his courtiers, with the exception of the Muhammadan Fakírs, were ready to please him by joining in his drinking bouts and indeed were habitually as drunken as himself. But with all this hard drinking, which was the custom of his age and country and should not be regarded as anything unusual, the Mahárájá was always fit for business at the proper and assigned time. Every foreign visitor to his Court was struck with his intelligence, eager curiosity, and general information, and there was nothing of which he was fonder than to discuss the manners and constitutions of other countries and to hear about the armies and campaigns of Europe. His manners to strangers were particularly pleasing and courteous, and many accounts are extant by travellers, who visited Lahore during the latter years of his reign, which attest the fascination he exercised over those in immediate relation to him.

Like most men who have been distinguished in history for administrative vigour and military genius, Ranjít Singh was very susceptible to feminine influence. His experiences were not however such as to give a favourable impression of the manners and morals of the ladies of the Punjab. His grandmother, Mai Desan, was killed by his father for an intrigue with a Bráhman; and Ranjít Singh is said to have killed his own mother Ráni Ráj Kour, popularly known as Mai Malwai, for a similar offence. Of his own wives and mistresses, the chronicle is too scandalous for more than passing mention in this place. When he had secured the legitimate succession in the person of his son Kharak Singh, he cared little for the discreditable intrigues of his harem. Many children were fathered upon him by these ladies, either for political objects or in the hope of obtaining his special favour; and although the astute Mahárájá was never deceived, he generally accepted the children as his own, with a certain grim amusement, and would ask why fortune had favoured him in so extraordinary a manner. To his son, Kharak Singh, and to his grandson, Nao Nihál Singh, he sent several ladies of more than doubtful reputation from his own zenána; one of these being the beautiful Isar Kour, who was so cruelly forced to become *Satí* on the death of Mahárájá Kharak Singh.

Ranjít Singh married eighteen wives; nine by the orthodox ceremonial and nine by the simpler rite of throwing the sheet, which has been already described. Only a few of these require any special notice[1].

Mahtab Kour was the first in order, married in 1786, a match which gave Ranjít Singh his commanding position, she being the granddaughter and heiress of the powerful Kanheya baron Jai Singh. Her mother, the widow Sada Kour, a truly remarkable woman, who realized that if her daughter was to retain her influence she must present her husband with an heir, procured a boy during one of the Mahárájá's expeditions and passed him off as her daughter's. The child, named Ishar Singh, only lived a year and a half; and Sada Kour determined to try the effect of twins. When Ranjít Singh had started on his Cis-Sutlej expedition of 1807, it was given out that Mahtab Kour was pregnant, and on his return twin sons were presented to him, one purchased from a chintz-weaver, and the other the offspring of a slave-girl in Mai Sada Kour's house. Ranjít Singh at first refused to have anything to say to the children, but the following year, when he was almost at war

[1] The full details of all the wives and children, real and reputed, of Mahárájá Ranjít Singh, his son, grandson, and successors, will be found in *The Punjab Chiefs*.

with the English over the Cis-Sutlej question, he thought it necessary to conciliate his terrible mother-in-law who had the Rámgarhia barons at her back, and acknowledged the boys, treating them as his own and allowing them the title of Prince. One of them, Tara Singh, was an idiot; the other, Sher Singh, grew up an exceedingly handsome, brave and stupid man, and succeeded to the throne after the death of Nao Nihál Singh, but was assassinated in 1843 by the Sindhanwalia chiefs.

The second wife of the Mahárájá was Ráj Kour, the daughter of Rám Singh, a Nakkai chief. She was married in 1798, and four years later gave birth to Kharak Singh, who was the only child, legitimate or illegitimate, by a wife or a slave-girl, ever born to Ranjít Singh. Kharak Singh succeeded his father without opposition, but was a man of weak intellect and was no more than a puppet in the hands of his ambitious son, Nao Nihál Singh, and the intriguing Rájás of Jammu, who poisoned him when they had had enough of him. Nao Nihál Singh, in his turn, was assassinated as he was returning from his father's cremation.

The other wives were of less importance. One, whom the Mahárájá married in 1833, in orthodox fashion and with great splendour, was a courtesan named Gul Begam of Amritsar city. When still a young man, in 1806, a yet more famous woman of the same professional courtesan class, named Morán, obtained great influence over him, and Ranjít Singh was not ashamed to parade, very drunk, on an elephant, during the Holi festival, with Morán by his side. She obtained a grant of Firozpur, and sent troops to reduce it, though without success; and coins, with her name and effigy, were struck in caricature of the East India Company which, in popular Indian belief, was a woman.

Another woman who rose to fame, or rather to notoriety, after the death of the great Mahárájá, was Jindan, the reputed mother of Mahárájá Dhulíp Singh. She was the daughter of Manna Singh, a trooper in the service of the palace, and as a clever mimic and dancer she attracted the notice of the old Mahárájá and was taken into the zenána, where her open intrigues caused astonishment even in the easy Lahore Court. A menial servant, a water-carrier, of the name of Gulu, was generally accepted as the father of Dhulíp Singh. At any rate, the father was not Mahárájá Ranjít Singh, who was paralysed several years before the birth of the child. Nor did he ever marry Jindan by formal or informal marriage. Many believed that Dhulíp Singh was not born of Jindan at all; but was brought into the palace to favour an intrigue of the Jammu Rájás, Ghuláb Singh and Dhyán Singh, who required a child to put forward when all the other possible heirs, real or reputed, of the Mahárájá should have perished; and it is certain that Jindan and the child were for some time sheltered at Jammu and only produced at a convenient time. However this may be, in the wild anarchy which succeeded the death of Sher Singh, when all the scum of the pot rose to the surface, Jindan, with her last professed lover, Rájá Lál Singh, played a conspicuous and infamous part, and her debaucheries and her unworthy paramour were in large part the cause of the Sutlej war and the ruin of the Sikh kingdom. Dhulip Singh, a child of nine years, was the titular Mahárájá when the British army reached Lahore after the campaign; and as it was convenient to accept the *status quo*, and as a nominal ruler was required for a country which the English Government had then no desire to annex or permanently occupy, the reputed child of the servant-maid and the water-carrier was confirmed on the throne of the Lion of the Punjab. Fortune, with her ever-turning wheel, must have laughed at the transformation.

CHAPTER VI

The Court of Ranjít Singh

A dry record of the campaigns fought by the Maháráj, the principalities he annexed and the chiefs he overthrew, would have little interest for the English reader, who rather desires to know what manner of man the Maháráj was; by what means and instruments he obtained his astonishing success, and what was the character of the chiefs who surrounded him. An attempt will be made in this chapter to give portraits of the principal courtiers of the Maháráj, some of which were drawn by me many years ago when the originals they represent were still alive, or from the faithful accounts given to me by their sons or companions[1].

The Maháráj was far too astute a man to trouble himself about the antecedents of his subordinate officials. So long as a man did him good service in the cabinet or the field, he was trusted and rewarded. As soon as he found his confidence betrayed, or the instrument he had chosen inefficient or unworthy, he

[1] In *The Punjab Chiefs*.

threw it contemptuously aside; so contemptuously that he often did not deign to punish the offender. But, generally, looking at the career of the Mahárájá from the time that he securely established his throne after the capture of Múltán in 1818, it is astonishing to see with what fidelity he was served and how few of his officials turned against him. It is true, little was to be gained by revolt or treachery, for in every department of the State corruption was the rule. Officials might squeeze the peasantry at their pleasure so long as they paid their due proportion of the revenue into the royal treasury. The only limit to oppression was the resistance of the people which, in the hot-blooded Punjab, is certain to occur at a known and fixed point of the political thermometer. The Ját Sikh, or the Muhammadan of the Jehlam district, will not endure more than the normal and traditional amount of official robbery; when more than this was attempted, his hand and those of his clansmen flew to their swords and a good deal of trouble was the result.

The Sikh Sirdárs were granted estates liable to feudal military service, and they maintained in addition a motley crew of armed followers of their own, and a princely state within their own districts. To many of them were also assigned tracts of country to administer, although administration meant little more than the collection of the Government revenue. In these cases the whole work fell on the money-lender and the Bráhman land-agent, to whom the Sikh Sirdár assigned his responsibilities, deducting a large commission for himself; how much, his master rarely cared to inquire. As it was then in the Punjab so is it to-day in some of the Feudatory States of India. There are many vast estates granted to his courtiers by the late Maháráját Sindhia, which were never visited by the assignees, who only asked that the rents should be regularly transmitted to Gwalior. On these distant properties every villainy and oppression was common: all financial and judicial control being in the hands of some greedy Bráhman or Baniyá on a nominal salary, who waxed rich on what he stole from his master and plundered from the people.

Mahárájá Ranjít Singh was a superstitious but not a religious man. His wild youth and stormy manhood had left him neither the leisure nor the inclination to master the metaphysical niceties of Guru Nának or to follow the complicated rules of conduct enjoined by Guru Govind Singh. He was an opportunist, to whom only those doctrines were agreeable which allowed him to rivet his authority more closely on the rude Játs he ruled. Thus he gave large gifts, on convenient occasions, to Sikh temples and priests; and several of the most influential of the religious leaders, Bábás and Bhais, found an honourable place at his court. Nor did these holy men, who were but half educated at the best, and who understood the mysticism of Nának as little as the Sikh priests of to-day, care much for orthodoxy so long as they were well paid for acquiescence in heterodoxy. The main idea of Sikhism was the destruction of Islám, and it was unlawful to salute Muhammadans, to associate with them, or to make peace with them on any terms. But several of the most trusted of the Maháráján's ministers were of this hated creed. Even the employment of Bráhmans was expressly forbidden by Govind Singh, who had been cast out and denounced by this spiritual aristocracy of Hinduism for his abolition of caste and denial of their authority. Yet Jamadár Khushhál Singh, Rájá Tej Singh, Rájá Sáhib Dyál, Rájá Rallia Rám, Diwán Ajodhia Parshád, Pandit Shunkar Nath, and numerous other prominent Darbár officials were Bráhmans. The tolerance of the Maháráján was due rather to indifference and selfishness than to any enlightened sentiment, and it may be doubted whether religious toleration has any securer basis in any time or country. Intolerance is born of strong passionate beliefs; and fanaticism only dies out as doubt enters, and the fire of religious enthusiasm burns low. But whatever its origin, the liberalism of the Maháráján had an excellent effect upon his administration, and his example was at once followed by other Sikh States. To-day there is no sign of the old intolerance favoured by Govind—an intolerance quite as ferocious as that of Muhammadanism itself. The greatest of the Sikh Principalities of the Cis-Sutlej, that of Patiála, has during the last three reigns been admirably served in the offices of Prime Minister and Foreign Secretary by two Muhammadan gentlemen, Khalifas Syad Muhammad Hassan, and Syad Muhammad

Hussain, who, for ability, integrity, and accomplishments, have no superiors in any native Court; while in the Sikh States of Kapúrthala, Nábha, and Jínd, officials of the same creed hold places of honour and responsibility. As to Bráhmans, it is doubtful whether the rules of Guru Govind Singh ever passed beyond the authority of a pious opinion; for the weight of the Hindu theocracy bore heavily on the necks of all who had once been subjected to it, and the most audacious among the Sikhs could not openly outrage the popular sentiment in favour of the sanctity of the Bráhman. But whatever the rules of Sikhism might enjoin, it was virtually impossible to carry on a complex administration without making use of the only classes, Muhammadans and Bráhmans, who had any hereditary capacity for government.

Democracies may assert the equality of intellect and extol the *carrière ouverte aux talents*, but the practice of Republics in Europe and America gives the doctrine the lie. Governing is an art which may no doubt be brilliantly practised without special training by some men of exceptional genius; but, as an ordinary accomplishment, it must be painfully and laboriously acquired, while hereditary aptitude and the class and family traditions of rule are very important factors in its success. Now, to the Bráhmans and the Muhammadans alone did the hereditary talent of government belong in the days of Ranjít Singh. The former had created the existing Hindu system of polity, and while to the fighting class they had cleverly assigned the glory and danger of kingship, they had retained the substantial power in their own hands. They were the spiritual guides and the worldly advisers of the monarch; their authority overshadowed his; he reigned and they governed. So with the Muhammadans. For several hundred years, by invasion and conquest, they had ruled India as a military Empire; and although they were no more able to dispense with the inevitable Bráhman than the Hindu monarchs they superseded, yet Muhammadan Emperors were naturally served largely by officials of their own creed, who had either originally accompanied the army of invasion or had descended from its chiefs and officials; while the great majority of Hindu converts to Islám who obtained profitable employment were the most intelligent of the Hindu community, for to accept the creed of the conqueror is an obvious proof of exceptional astuteness.

Against the cultured intelligence of these races what had the poor Ját cultivator, as stupid as his own buffaloes, to oppose? Not to him the triumphs of diplomacy and the conflict of quick intellects in the atmosphere of a court. He could do no more than plough straight and fight. In an intellectual competition with Bráhmans and Muhammadans he was as a cart-horse matched against thoroughbreds. Mahárájá Ranjít Singh recognised this truth very early in his career. It was pressed on him, in 1807, by Sirdár Fateh Singh Kálianwala, before mentioned, when he lay dying of a wound received in the unsuccessful storm of Náráyangarh. The chief is said to have counselled him never to appoint any Ját Sikh to a position of authority about the court, but to confine them to military service. Whether the story be true or not it is certain that the Mahárájá observed the principle and, while his bravest officers and generals were Játs, in the council he gave his confidence to Bráhmans, Rájputs, Muhammadans: or even to Khattrís, like Diwán Sáwan Mall. As it was then so it is at the present time. Two generations of British rule have not modified in any essential particular the character of the Ját Sikhs. They are still as impatient of education, as slow witted, as simple in their habits and ideas as when Ranjít Singh formed them, for a few years, into the semblance of a nation.

The most conspicuous figure in the eyes of foreigners visiting the court of the Mahárájá was Fakír Azizuddin, his Foreign Minister. He, with his brothers Nuruddin and Imámuddin, was descended from a Muhammadan family of Bokhára of great respectability, and in that country many of his descendants still reside. His father, Ghulám Mohaiuddin, was a clever medical practitioner. In 1799 the principal Lahore physician, with whom Azizuddin was studying, placed the youth in attendance on Ranjít Singh, when that chief, soon after his capture of Lahore, was suffering from ophthalmia. The skill and attention of the young doctor won the chief's regard. Azizuddin received a grant of several villages, was appointed personal physician to the Mahárájá, and as Ranjit's territories increased the wealth and estates of Azizuddin grew also. It was his wise influence in 1808 which prevented Ranjit Singh from declaring war with the British, when they first curbed his power by confining his conquests to the north of the Sutlej. The Mahárájá was so convinced of the wisdom of Azizuddin's advice on this occasion that he never undertook any serious operations without consulting him. In all matters connected with Europeans and the English Government Azizuddin was specially employed, and to his enlightened and liberal counsels it may be attributed that throughout his long reign the Mahárájá maintained such close friendship with the English Government. Trusting implicitly to its good faith, he would set out with his whole army on distant expeditions, leaving only the Fakír with a few orderlies for the protection of Lahore. Azizuddin was occasionally employed on military service, and whenever it was necessary to send a special embassy, as to Lord William Bentinck in 1831 and to Amir Dost Muhammad in 1835, the Fakír was always selected and was always equal to the emergency. On the historical occasion of the Mahárájá's meeting with the Governor-General at Rúpar in 1831, which has been called the meeting of 'the field of cloth of gold,' and on the equally memorable and magnificent visit to Lord Auckland at Firozpur in 1838, the most onerous part of the duties fell to the share of Fakír Azizuddin. He was one of the ablest and certainly the most honest of all Ranjít Singh's courtiers.

Azizuddin was of so engaging a disposition, and so perfect a courtier in his manners, that he made few declared enemies, though many were doubtless jealous of his influence. One reason of his popularity, as a Muhammadan minister at a Hindu Court, was the liberality of his belief. He was a Sufi, a sect held, indeed, as infidel by orthodox Muhammadans, but to which the best thinkers and poets of the East have belonged. He had no love for the barren dogmata of the Kurán, but looked on all religions as equally to be respected and disregarded. On one occasion Ranjít Singh asked him whether he preferred the Hindu or the Muhammadan religion. 'I am,' he replied, 'a man floating in the midst of a mighty river. I turn my eyes towards the land, but can distinguish no difference in either bank.' He was celebrated as the most eloquent man of his day, and he was as able with his pen as with his tongue. The state papers drawn up by him are models of elegance and good taste, according to the Oriental standard. He was himself a ripe scholar in all branches of Eastern science, and was also a generous and discriminating patron of learning. At Lahore he founded at his own expense a College for the study of Persian and Arabic, and to this institution many of the Arabic scholars of the Punjab of the past generation owed their training.

As a poet Azizuddin may be allowed a high place. His Persian verses, of the mystical character which the Sufis affect, are often beautiful, and distinguished by simplicity and great elegance of style. A few stanzas, literally translated, are inserted here to show the character of Sufi religious poetry:—

'If you attentively regard the world
You will find it fugitive as a shadow:
Why should you vex yourself with vain desires
When you have no power to perform?
Forget yourself, and leave your work with God;
Trust yourself with all confidence to Him.
Wait with patience until He shall bless you,
And thank Him for what He has already given.
Stop your ears from the sound of earthly care;
Rejoice in God and be hopeful of His mercy.
The wise would consider me as an idolater
Should I thoughtlessly speak of myself as "*I*";
To the wise and to those who most nearly know,
It is a folly for any mortal to assert "*I am*";
Although able to vanquish Sahrab, Zal, and Rustam,
Yet at the last your stability is but as water.
It is a vain thought that your reason may spin
His imaginings, as a spider spins her web.
It is well that I should breathe the air of freedom,
For I know that everything is dependent upon God.'

The elaborately polished manners of Fakír Azizuddin, and his exaggeration of flattery and compliment, struck foreigners the more strangely at so rough and rude a court as that of Lahore. What was the natural atmosphere in the courtly Muhammadan circles at Bokhára and Delhi seemed somewhat grotesque in the Minister of an illiterate Sikh chief. On Baron Charles Hügel, who travelled in the Punjab in 1835–36, and whose narrative is perhaps the most delightful of any which have been written on that country previous to its annexation, the personality of the Fakír made an immense impression, and he gives many instances of his flowery discourse. He, as usual, was the intermediary between the Mahárájá and his European guest, who was almost persuaded to accept the Mahárájá's service on the princely salary of Rs. 6000 a month, the ability and accomplishments of the young traveller having aroused the Mahárájá's surprise. It is evident that the Baron entertained a sincere admiration for the Minister, in spite of his extravagant compliments, which were, after all, no more than the habitual conversational currency of the Persian language.

In 1842, Azizuddin, having been deputed to meet Lord Ellenborough at Firozpur, where a grand Darbár was to be held, explained away an apparent discourtesy in the failure of the Sikh envoy to meet the Governor-General with such courtesy and ability that the Governor-General declared him in full Darbár to be 'the protector of the friendship of both States' and presented him with his own gold watch, which I have often seen in the possession of his son, who was for several years one of my secretaries at Lahore[1]. Fakír Azizuddin died in December, 1845, just before the crushing defeats of the first Sikh War. With his dying

[1] Sayad Jamáluddin, Mir Munshi, Secretariat.

breath he protested against the march of the Sikh army to the Sutlej; performing, though in vain, his last service to both the English and the Lahore States. Of all his family, many of whom I have known, his nephew Shamshuddin most resembled him. He is now dead, but for many years I enjoyed his intimate friendship, and I have never in India met a man of more refined manners, or a greater flow of eloquence of the florid Persian order. The younger brothers of Azizuddin, Imamuddin and Nuruddin, were both important members of the Maháráјá's Court, although their position was not so conspicuous as that of their elder brother. Nuruddin especially enjoyed a very general respect in the country, and, after the war of 1846, when Rájá Lál Singh was deposed for treason, Nuruddin was appointed one of the Council of Regency to carry on the administration until the majority of the infant Maháráјá Dhulíp Singh. The elder brother was ordinarily known at court by the title of the Fakír Sáhib; not that the style of Fakír which the family were proud enough to retain signified, as the word ordinarily implies, any vow of poverty, for the brothers were all wealthy. Nuruddin was known at court as the Khalifa Sáhib, and Imamuddin was, during the greater portion of Ranjít Singh's reign, and until the time of Maháráјá Sher Singh, governor of the important fortress of Govindgarh, which commanded the city of Amritsar.

Two prominent Muhammadans at court were the Nawáb Sarafráz Khán of Múltán and his younger brother Zu-l-fakár Khán, sons of the stout old chief Muzaffar Khán, who had died sword in hand, with five of his sons and a large number of his clan, defending the breach when Ranjít assaulted and captured the fortress and city. No victory of the Mahárájá had been more fiercely disputed or so hardly won as this; and when his power was securely established over the Múltán province, he had the generosity to treat the sons of his vanquished enemy with kindness and consideration. He brought them to Lahore and settled pensions upon them, which were continued to their representatives by the British Government.

Another of the conquered Muhammadan chiefs who figured in Ranjít Singh's train at Lahore was Khudá Yár Khán, the Tiwána chief who, with his cousins, was brought to Lahore in command of fifty Tiwána horse, the boldest riders and the most picturesque looking men to be found anywhere in the Punjab. The Tiwánas have always been famous for their gallant bearing, and under English officers have done splendid service.

One of the most conspicuous figures at the Mahárájá's Court was Jamadár Khushhál Singh. He was the son of a Bráhman shopkeeper in the Meerut district. At the age of seventeen he came to Lahore to seek his fortune and was taken into the Dhonkal Singhwala Regiment, then newly raised, on five rupees a month. He soon made friends with the Mahárájá's chamberlains, and was placed on the personal guard of Ranjít Singh. Here, by his vigilance, aided by good looks and soldierly bearing, he attracted the favourable notice of the Mahárájá. The story told by the family is that one night Ranjít Singh went out in disguise, and on his return to the palace was stopped by Khushhál, who was on guard, and who detained his master in the watch-house till morning, and that this vigilance pleased the Mahárájá so much that he kept Khushhál by him as a personal attendant. However this may be, it is certain that he rose daily in his master's favour till, in 1811, he was appointed *Deorhiwala* or chamberlain, with the title of Jamadár. The appointment was one of importance. The chamberlain was master of the ceremonies, regulated processions, and superintended the Darbár. It was through him alone that any individual, however high in rank, could obtain a private interview with the Mahárájá, although the daily Darbár was open to all men of family or official importance.

Five years after he arrived at Lahore he was baptized as a Sikh, and after this grew rapidly in favour and became very wealthy; as his influence with his master was used to obtain bribes and contributions from all attending the court. He was employed on various military duties, and in 1832 was appointed governor of Kashmír under Prince Sher Singh, where his oppression converted a year of scarcity into one of famine. He was not a man of any particular ability, and although the Mahárájá is said to have been attracted by his good looks in the first instance, yet his portraits taken later in life present him as a coarse, vulgar looking man, far inferior to the handsome Sikh Sirdárs. He was unpopular at court, and always showed himself something of a tyrant.

His nephew, Tej Singh, who followed him to Lahore, also rose to favour and was made a Rájá. He was commander-in-chief of the Sikh army during the first campaign with the English, and was accused both of treachery and cowardice. But the temper of the Sikh army was so suspicious, and the circumstances under which he held command were so difficult, that those who have most carefully examined the action of Tej Singh at the time are inclined to acquit him of anything beyond vacillation and weakness.

The most famous of the fighting chiefs, and the one to whom the Mahárájá was most attached, was Harí Singh Nalwa, who was born, like Ranjít Singh himself, at the town of Gujránwála. He was not only the bravest, but the most skilful of all the Mahárájá's generals, and was employed to command all expeditions of exceptional difficulty. He was chiefly instrumental in the capture of Múltán in 1818, and in the following year he commanded a division of the army invading Kashmír, of which country he was afterwards appointed governor; but his talents did not lie in the direction of administration, and he became so unpopular that the Mahárájá was compelled to recall him. After this he was chiefly employed on the Punjab frontier as governor of Hazára, and subsequently of Pesháwar, where, in 1837, he was slain in a pitched battle with the Afgháns.

After Harí Singh Nalwa, the most conspicuous fighting chief was Sirdár Attar Singh Sindhanwalia, who from his strength and courage was considered the champion of the Khálsa. He was a member of the most powerful family in the Punjab proper, that to which the Mahárájá himself belonged. The Sindhanwalias were a turbulent race, and Attar Singh, his brother Lehna Singh, and his nephew Ajit Singh were all conspicuous in the intrigues which preceded and followed the death of Ranjít Singh. They represented the opposition to the power and influence of the three Jammu Rájás, and all died violent deaths.

Rájá Guláb Singh, Rájá Dhyán Singh and Rájá Suchet Singh, were of a Dogra Rájput family of humble origin, but by sheer force of character and ability, rose to great power during the latter days of the monarchy. Rájá Dhyán Singh, the second brother, was, during the Mahárájá's lifetime, the most important of the three. He succeeded Jamadár Khushhál Singh in charge of the Deorhi, and was virtually for some years Prime Minister, being the channel of communication between the Mahárájá and the people, and having general control of all departments except those of finance and foreign affairs, which were respectively in the hands of Rájá Dina Náth and Fakír Azizuddin. His brother, Guláb Singh, was generally employed on military duties, but after the death of the Mahárájá and the murder of his brother, Dhyán

Singh, he became for a time the most important person in the Lahore State, and his services to the British during the first Sutlej campaign were such that he was granted the independent sovereignty of the Province of Kashmir by the Governor-General. There are, perhaps, no characters in Punjab history more repulsive than Rájás Dhyán Singh and Guláb Singh; their splendid talents and undoubted bravery only render more conspicuous their atrocious cruelty, their treachery, their avarice, and their unscrupulous ambition. The third brother, Suchet Singh, was the handsomest man in the Sikh army and a very splendid figure at court. He had little of the ability of his brothers, and played altogether a subordinate part in Lahore politics. Rájá Híra Singh, the nephew of Rájá Dhyán Singh, was a young man of great promise; he succeeded his father as Prime Minister, but like him, was assassinated during the troubles which preceded the first Sikh War.

Among the men who rose to power during the latter days of the Mahárájá's life, no one was more remarkable than Rájá Dina Náth. He has been well and happily styled the Talleyrand of the Punjab, and his life and character bear a strong resemblance to those of the European statesman. Revolutions in which his friends and patrons perished passed him by; dynasties rose and fell but never involved him in their ruin; in the midst of bloodshed and assassination his life was never endangered; while confiscation and judicial robbery were the rule of the State, his wealth and power continually increased. His sagacity and far-sightedness were such, that when, to other eyes, the political sky was clear, he could perceive the signs of a coming storm which warned him to desert a losing party or a falling friend. Honest men do not survive many revolutions, and the Rájá's falseness was the measure of his success. He was patriotic, but his love of country was subordinate to his love of self. He hated the English with a bitter hatred, for they were stronger than he or his country; but his interests compelled him to serve, like Samson, the Philistines he hated. He was not without his own notions of fidelity, and would stand by a friend as long as he could do so with safety to himself. Even when he deserted him it was more from thoughts of danger to his wealth and influence than from personal fear, for Rájá Dina Náth was physically brave, and also possessed, in an eminent degree, moral courage; though it did not lead him to do right regardless of consequences. He possessed immense local knowledge and as vast a capacity for work; but his desire of keeping power in his own hands had an evil effect on the progress of business. He was an accomplished man of the world, courteous and considerate; well educated, though nothing of a scholar, and in conversation with Europeans he would express himself with a boldness and apparent candour that were as pleasant as they are unusual in Asiatics.

It was only in 1834 that Rájá Dina Náth was made Finance Minister, for which his qualifications were exceedingly high, but the Maháráját had for many years reposed great confidence in him, and he was on all occasions of importance one of his most trusted advisers. After the death of his master he retained great influence with the chiefs and the army, and on the British occupation of Lahore was appointed to the Council of Regency, of which he was a most able and useful member. Although his position at the head of the Financial Department gave him many opportunities of enriching himself at the public expense, of which there is every reason to believe he availed himself, he still worked more disinterestedly than others, and was of great service to the Resident at Lahore. Without his clear head and business-like habits it would have been almost impossible to disentangle the Darbár accounts, and after the annexation of the Punjab Dina Náth's aid in revenue and jagír matters was almost as valuable as before. At the time of the revolt of the Sikh army in 1848, it was asserted by some that Rájá Dina Náth was a traitor at heart; that he had himself encouraged the rising; and that had he not been a wealthy man, with houses and gardens and many lakhs of rupees in Lahore, convenient for confiscation, he would have joined the rebels without hesitation; but these stories were perhaps invented by his enemies. Certain it is that on his being recalled to Lahore he zealously carried out the wishes of the British authorities in confiscating the property of the rebels and in counteracting their schemes.

Among the constant, though generally silent attendants in Darbár, must be mentioned the Sikh priests, Bhai Rám Singh, Bhai Govind Rám and Bhai Gúrmukh Singh. The first two of these were the grandsons of a famous Sikh priest and prophet who lived at Lahore, the object of universal respect on the part of the Sikhs during the greater part of the eighteenth century, and who died at nearly a hundred years of age, two years after the Maháráj́á captured the city of Lahore in 1802. Ranjít Singh had the greatest respect for this holy man and granted estates to his grandsons. Of these, Rám Singh had the most influence, and during a campaign his tent was regularly pitched next to that of Ranjít Singh. A messenger from the Maháráj́á was always sent to escort them to Darbár, and they were treated with high honour. Bhai Gúrmukh Singh was the son of Sant Singh, the guardian of the sacred temple of the Darbár Sáhib at Amritsar, who had been a soldier as well as a priest and served with the army on several occasions with great credit. When he gave up worldly affairs and devoted himself to the reading and expounding of the Sikh scriptures, he sent his son Gúrmukh Singh to court. The youth soon became as great a favourite as his father had been, although his influence was never equal to that of his enemy and rival, Bhai Rám Singh.

Other men of importance at Lahore were Misr Rallia Rám, Chief of the Customs Department, with his son, afterwards Rájá Sáhib Dyál; the Sirdárs of the great house of Attáriwala, Sirdárs Chatar Singh, Sher Singh and Shám Singh; the two former of whom were the principal leaders of the Sikh rebellion in 1848; the Sirdárs of the house of Majíthia, of whom Sirdár Desa Singh and his son Sirdár Lehna Singh were the most conspicuous. Lehna Singh was known as *Hasmuddaula*, the Sword of the State, and was a man of considerable ability. He was a skilful mechanist and an original inventor. He much improved the Sikh ordnance, and some very beautiful guns of his manufacture were taken at Aliwál and elsewhere. Among other things he invented a clock which showed the hour, the day of the month, and the changes of the moon. He was fond of astronomy and mathematics and was master of several languages. As an administrator he was very popular. The poor were never oppressed by him, his assessments were moderate and his decisions essentially just. As a statesman, he may be said to have been almost the only honest man in Lahore. Fraud and corruption were supreme, but the hands of Lehna Singh were always clean: surrounded by the most greedy and unscrupulous of schemers, he preserved his honesty unsullied.

Had a man of the reputation and administrative talent of Lehna Singh taken the lead in 1845 in the Punjab, the great troubles which came upon the country might have been averted. But he was no true patriot. He did not understand that the religion of a statesman, and indeed of every honest man, is to stand by his country in times of danger, sharing her griefs and, if need be, falling with her fall.

CHAPTER VII

The Army and Administration of the Mahárájá

The military genius of Mahárájá Ranjít Singh was not so much shown in his generalship, for in this he was surpassed by many of his officers and Sirdárs, as in the skill with which he formed a powerful, disciplined, and well equipped army out of the raw Sikh levies, turbulent and independent, who had been accustomed to carry their swords from one leader to another as they saw the best chance of plunder, and who changed their masters as often as it suited their inclination or convenience.

When his grandfather, Charrat Singh, and his father, Mahán Singh, had command of the Sukarchakia confederacy, the Sikhs were a thoroughly republican body. Chiefs and leaders arose with more or less authority, as was inevitable in anarchic days, when every man owned what he could take by force and hold against all comers, but this leadership gave no man a more intrinsically honourable position in the eyes of the people. The Sikh theocracy had equality and fraternity for its foundations far more literally than has been the case with the modern republics of Europe and America.

An account of the organisation and system of fighting of the Sikhs has been given in a preceding chapter. They were essentially horsemen, not footmen. The infantry soldier was considered altogether inferior to the cavalry, and was, in time of war, left behind to garrison forts, to look after the women, or to follow, as best he could, the fighting force, until he, in his turn, could afford to change his status and buy or steal a horse for his own use.

Mahárájá Ranjít Singh, very early in his career, recognised, with his usual sagacity, that the Sikh system was unsuited to the genius of the people, and that until it was modified he could not hope to win solid victories over regular troops like the English, whose drill and tactics he studied with infinite patience, or even over the Afgháns, who in the time of Ahmad Sháh were fairly disciplined, and formidable opponents even in the open country, while in the hills they were almost invincible. When he had thoroughly mastered the secret of the superiority of the British organization, against which all the military races of India had tried their strength in vain, he resolved to create an army on similar lines, while he determined, not less resolutely, to keep peace with the only power which he had learned to respect. With these ideas, the Mahárájá changed the entire organisation of the Khálsa army. The cavalry ceased to be the most important arm, and the infantry became the favourite service. The change was facilitated by the employment of European officers, French and Italian, whom the Mahárájá engaged when he failed to obtain the loan of officers of the East India Company's service. These foreign generals introduced the system which had become general in Europe, where the value of infantry as against cavalry was universally acknowledged. Some of them were men of considerable ability and quite competent to perform all they promised in increasing the efficiency of the Lahore army. The infantry under their instruction became a most formidable body of troops, well disciplined and steady, though slow in manœuvring. Their endurance was very great, and a whole regiment would march 30 miles a day for many days together.

Enlistment in the regular army during the Mahárájá's reign was entirely voluntary, but there was no difficulty in obtaining recruits, for the service was exceedingly popular. The cavalry was constituted much in the same manner as in the early days of the Khálsa, when clouds of horsemen hung on the skirts of the Afghán armies, afraid to venture an attack upon regular troops, but cutting off convoys, and endangering the communications of the enemy. This is no doubt one of the principal duties of light horse; but the Sikh cavalry were, as a rule, miserably mounted and armed, and became more celebrated for taking to flight when attacked than for any display of valour. On foot the Sikh is the bravest and steadiest of soldiers; but on horseback, although there are some crack cavalry regiments of Sikhs in the English service that can hold their own with any horsemen in the world, they are surpassed by Afgháns and Hindustánis who are inferior to them as infantry. In the Mahárájá's army the infantry were the pick of the youth of the country; only the handsomest and strongest men were selected, while the cavalry were irregular troops, the contingents of his different Sirdárs, and not appointed for any considerations of bravery or strength. The horses were small, weak, and ill-bred, and the accoutrements were of the roughest and coarsest kind. In the armies of the Sikh States at the present day, all of which I have often reviewed and inspected, and one of which it was my duty to reorganise, the same practice prevails. The infantry are in size and physique equal to the Sikhs in the British army: while the cavalry regiments have been turned into a hospital for old and decrepit pensioners, who can sit on a horse, although they cannot fight or perform any service requiring bodily exertion.

I have already referred to the Akális as the only infantry soldiers who, in the old Khálsa days, enjoyed any consideration. The Mahárájá was afraid to interfere too closely with these men; for though little better than drunken savages, they were supposed by the Sikhs to possess a semi-sacred character, and were, moreover, useful when desperate deeds were to be done which the rank and file of the army might have declined. They nearly embroiled the Mahárájá with the English by their fanatical attack upon Mr. Metcalfe's Mussulman escort in 1809[1], and their reckless valour turned many a wavering fight into a victory. They were identical in character and in the manner of their onslaught with the Gházis of Afghánistán and the Soudán, whose fierce and terrible attack shakes the nerves of all but the steadiest and most seasoned troops; but the Sikh soldiers of God drew their courage more from drink and maddening drugs, than from the depths of religious enthusiasm which inspires the wild children of Islám. They were an unmitigated nuisance and danger during the Mahárájá's reign, and more than once they attempted his life.

Their insolent swagger and hatred to Europeans made them so obnoxious during the early years of the British occupation and annexation, that visits to the Temple of the Darbár Sáhib at Amritsar, where the Akál Bungah formed their head-quarters, were always attended with some risk. The Mahárájá was tolerant or indifferent, and desired his Muhammadan subjects to perform their ceremonial without molestation, yet it was found necessary to prohibit the call to prayer of the *Muezzin*, as it roused the Akális to fury. The Mahárájá tried to reduce these fanatics to something like order by forming them into a corps of irregular cavalry, 3000 strong, but this had little

[1] The steadiness with which the Envoy's disciplined escort repulsed the raging mob of Akális made a great impression on Ranjít Singh, and not only disposed him to peace, but determined him to train and discipline his own troops in like fashion.

effect, and they always dismounted for a charge, in which the two-handed sword was their favourite weapon. The steel quoits, which they invariably wore on their turbans, six to eight inches in diameter, thin and with a sharp cutting edge, were not the formidable weapons they were pretended, and were as dangerous to friends as foes. I have never met an Akáli who could make good or sure practice with them, and I have often thrown against them with success. Their effective range is from sixty to one hundred yards.

Of the foreign officers who entered the Mahárájá's service General Ventura was the most important. He was an Italian of honour and reputation, who had served under Napoleon in the armies of Spain and Italy, and who, after the peace, finding his occupation gone, became a soldier of fortune ready for adventure in any part of the world. Of similar character and standing was General Allard, another of Napoleon's officers, who had won distinction by his ability and gallantry in many campaigns. These men first tried their fortune in Egypt and Persia, but finding no opening under Sháh Abbás, the ruling monarch, they travelled to India, viâ Herát and Kandahár, and were engaged by the Mahárájá after some hesitation and a prolonged examination of their qualifications. Both served Ranjít Singh long and faithfully. Allard was allowed to raise a corps of dragoons, and Ventura was placed in command of the *Fouj Khás* or special brigade, the first in rank, discipline and equipment in the Sikh army. Its normal strength was four infantry battalions and two regiments of cavalry, and although the Mahárájá at one time raised it to five battalions of infantry and three cavalry regiments, it was afterwards reduced, at Ventura's request, to its former numbers. In command of this force the general served in many campaigns with distinction, chiefly in the hills and around Peshávar. The Mahárájá always treated him with confidence and respect, and further appointed him Kázi and governor of Lahore, which gave him the third position in Darbár. Colonel Court, a Frenchman, educated at the École Polytechnique of Paris, commanded two battalions of Gúrkhas. Colonel Gardner was an Irishman, of less education and character, but of considerable ability, employed in the artillery[1]. Colonel Van Cortlandt was another officer, of mixed parentage, who on the downfall of the Sikh monarchy entered the service of the British Government in a civil capacity, and also performed excellent military service during the Mutiny. General Avitabile was a Neapolitan by birth, who came to Lahore some years later than Ventura, after service in Persia. He was generally employed in administrative work, first in charge of the Rechna

[1] Colonel Gardner has been dead for many years. When I knew him he was a pensioner, very rarely sober, of the late Mahárája of Kashmir. He allowed me to read his manuscript narrative of the later years of the Mahárájá, and the events which succeeded his death. These most interesting and valuable papers, which were entrusted to the late Mr. Frederick Cooper, C.B., have disappeared, and the loss from a historical point of view is considerable. (See p. 8.)

Doáb, the country between the rivers Rávi and Chenáb. Afterwards he held for some years the most troublesome charge in the Punjab, that of the Peshàwar district, where his stern and ferocious methods reduced that wild tract to something like order for the first time in its history. His name is still remembered with awe by the turbulent tribes in the neighbourhood of the Kháibar, numbers of whom, thieves and murderers, he hung around the walls of the city. His code of punishment was Draconian, and although the English rule is mild in comparison with that of this ferocious Italian, yet those who have to administer law and maintain order on the North-West Frontier of India must have a quick and heavy hand; and the slow and cumbrous procedure of High Courts and barrister judges is mere folly when compared with the gallop after a criminal, caught red-handed before he has reached his asylum in the hills, a short shrift and the nearest tree.

The foreign officers entertained by the Mahárájá, especially General Ventura in command of the Fouj Khás, and Court in charge of what was known as the French Legion, very much improved the discipline and tactical power of Ranjít Singh's army. They were not, however, entrusted with the supreme command in expeditions which was nominally given to one of the princes, Kharak Singh, or Sher Singh, or to one of the principal Sirdárs. Of all the generals of the Mahárájá, the best was probably Diwán Mokham Chand, a *khattrí* by birth, who from 1806 to 1814, when he died, was the virtual commander-in-chief of the Sikh army, and was associated with all his conquests. His grandson, Rám Dyál, killed in Hazára in 1820, was also a skilful commander, who would have risen to distinction if he had lived. Misr Diwán Chand, another Hindu of the trading class, and as such disliked by the Sikh Sirdárs, was the conqueror of Múltán in 1818, and the leader of the successful expedition against Kashmír in the following year. Among the Sikh chiefs who were most distinguished were Sirdár Fateh Singh Kálianwala; Sirdár Nihál Singh Attáriwála, who took a distinguished part in almost all the Mahárájá's campaigns from the year 1801 to 1817; Sirdár Fateh Singh Ahluwalia, the ancestor of the Kapúrthala Rájás; Sirdár Budh Singh Sindhanwalia, and his brother, Attar Singh, who, after the death of Sirdár Harí Singh Nalwa at Jamrúd in 1836, was considered the champion of the Khálsa. Harí Singh was a leader of infinite dash and gallantry, and was adored by the army; ever ready to fight and win, without counting the odds against him. His son, Jowáhir Singh, who was a great friend of mine, inherited all his father's valour, and it was he who led the splendid charge of irregular cavalry against the English at Chilianwála, which so nearly turned the victory into a catastrophe. I might mention the names of many other famous captains of the Mahárájá whose names are still household words in the Punjab, but they would have little interest to English readers.

As to the constitution of the Sikh army under Ranjit Singh and his successors, we have fairly exact information from the pay abstracts and returns found in the Lahore offices after the occupation in 1846. The composition of the Fouj Khás, which was under the command of General Ventura, may be taken as a specimen. He resigned in 1843, disgusted at the growing anarchy, and foreseeing the ruin which must ensue. It was not before he had received practical proof of the danger of remaining after the death of his master; for both he and General Court had been attacked by three regiments of the latter's battalion, and Ventura had been obliged to use his artillery to protect himself and his friend.

The Fouj Khás was composed, before the Sutlej War of 1845, as follows:—

Regular Infantry	3176
Regular Cavalry	1667
Artillery with 34 guns	855
	5698

The infantry force included the Khás battalion, strength 820 men; a Gúrkha battalion, 707 men; Dewa Singh's battalion, 839 men; and the Shám Sota battalion, 810 men.

The cavalry force was composed of a grenadier regiment, strength 730 men; a dragoon regiment, 750 men; and a troop of life guards, 187 men.

The artillery was the corps known as that of Iláhi

Baksh, and was commanded by a Mussulman general of that name, the best artillery officer in the Sikh army.

The pay of the whole brigade was Rs. 96,067 (then about £10,000) per mensem.

After the death of the Mahárájá in 1839, great changes occurred in the composition of the army. His strong hand had kept down mutiny and complaint, though even he was once constrained to take refuge in the fort of Govindgarh from the fury of a Gúrkha regiment which could not obtain its arrears of pay. His successors, fearing for their lives and power, were compelled to increase the numbers and pay of the army, till it at length became an insupportable burthen to the State and a standing menace to other Powers.

At the time of the Mahárájá's death the regular army, infantry, cavalry, and artillery, in numbers and monthly cost, as compared with the figures under his successors, stood as follows:—

	Number.	Guns.	Cost
1839 Mahárájá Ranjít Singh	29,168	192	Rs. 3,82,088
1840–43 Mahárájá Sher Singh	50,065	232	Rs. 5,48,603
1844 Rájá Hira Singh	50,805	282	Rs. 6,82,084
1845 Sirdár Jowáhir Singh	72,370	381	Rs. 8,52,696

The increase in the number of guns under Sirdár Jowáhir Singh was, in a great measure, nominal. Few new guns were cast, but many old ones were taken out of forts, furbished up, and placed on field carriages. The irregular cavalry does not appear to have increased in the same proportion as the regular army. At the commencement of the Sutlej War in 1845 its numbers were 16,292.

The roll of the army in the whole Punjab at that time was:—

Regular Infantry . . .	53,756
Regular Cavalry . . .	6,235
Irregular Cavalry . . .	16,292
Artillery	10,968
Camel Swivels . . .	584
Miscellaneous . . .	827
Total . .	88,662 men.

Guns—Field, 380; garrison, 104. Total 484. Camel swivels, 308.

The irregular levies and jagírdári contingents of horse, not included in the above, cannot be accurately determined, but they may be fairly estimated at 30,000 men. These formed the picturesque element in the Mahárájá's reviews. Many of the men were well-to-do country gentlemen, the sons, relations, or clansmen of the chiefs who placed them in the field and maintained them there, and whose personal credit was concerned in their splendid appearance. There was no uniformity in their dress. Some wore a shirt of mail, with a helmet inlaid with gold and a kalgi or heron's plume; others were gay with the many coloured splendours of velvet and silk, with pink or yellow muslin turbans, and gold embroidered belts carrying their sword and powder horn. All wore, at their back, the small round shield of tough buffalo hide. These magnificent horsemen were armed some with bows and arrows, but the majority with matchlocks, with which they made excellent practice.

The regular troops were much less picturesque than the jagírdári horse. Their dress was a close imitation of the scarlet uniforms worn by the British army, singularly ungraceful on native troops. Their pay compared favourably with that of the Company's troops—Rs. 10 per mensem for a foot-soldier—but on the other hand they received no pension; the cavalry received Rs. 25, but for this had to procure and maintain a horse and accoutrements.

An account of the civil administration under Mahárájá Ranjít Singh need not be lengthy, for I have already described it as the simple process of squeezing out of the unhappy peasant every rupee that he could be made to disgorge; the limit of oppression being only marked by the fear of his revolt or the abandonment of his land through discouragement and despair. The Sikh farmer of revenue did not wish to kill the goose that laid the golden eggs, but he plucked its feathers as closely as he dared. A few paragraphs from Land Revenue Settlement Reports will show how the Sikh procedure appeared in the eyes of the officers of the British Government, who administer a system which is as different from that of the Sikhs as light from darkness, and which indeed errs on the side of extravagant generosity. The British Government might largely increase the proportion which it claims of the rent of the land throughout large tracts of India without giving good grounds for reproach. In the Administration Report of the Punjab for 1872–73 I wrote as follows:—

'The Sikhs often actually took as much as one-half the gross produce of an estate, besides a multitude of cesses; our demand never exceeds one-sixth, is frequently not more than an eighth, a tenth, or a twelfth, and in some cases not more than a fifteenth of the average gross produce valued at average prices for a period of twenty to thirty years.'

The Customs Revenue in the latter days of Ranjít Singh realized Rs. 1,637,000, and the cost of collection was Rs. 110,000, or nearly 7 per cent. Duties were levied, under forty-eight heads, on almost every article of common use, without any attempt to discriminate between luxuries and necessaries, or to assess lightly the articles used by the poor, such as fuel, grain, or vegetables. The mode of collection was extremely vexatious, the country being covered with custom houses, at which merchants were treated with the utmost insolence and oppression. An article paid duty on being taken into a town, a second time on being taken to the shop, and a third time on re-export.

The following extracts from Settlement Reports have been collected by Mr. Ibbetson, and printed in his admirable Census Report for 1883. They express vividly and clearly the Sikh method of administration, and taken from various districts and different authorities, give a fairer estimate of the system than any single opinion could do [1].

First let us look to the frontier and Peshāwar. Capt. James writes as follows:—

'From 1800 to 1820, Peshāwar remained in a constant state of excitement and confusion, passing from one ruler to another, none of whom could exercise any real control over its wild occupants, and the hill tribes transferring their allegiance to the highest bidders. . . The periodical visits of the Sikhs were calamitous to the people; their approach was the signal for the removal of property and valuables, and even of the window and door-frames from the houses. Crowds of women and children fled frightened from their houses, and the country presented the appearance of an emigrating colony. As the hated host advanced they over-ran the neighbourhood, pillaging and destroying whatever came within their reach and laying waste the fields. There is scarce a village from the head of the valley to the Indus which has not been burnt and plundered by the Sikh Commander. His visitations were held in such awe that his name was used by mothers as a term of affright, to hush their unruly children, and at the present day, in travelling through the country, old greybeards, with many scars, point

[1] The Punjab Land Revenue Settlement Reports contain a vast amount of interesting information, social, fiscal, and historical, and are and will for ever remain a monument of the industry and ability of English administrative officers. Mr. Barnes' original Report on Kāngra is a literary work of great merit; so is the second Report on the same district by Sir J. B. Lyall. The Peshāwar Report by Capt. James is full of valuable information. Nothing that has been done in this direction in the Punjab, or other parts of India, surpasses in living interest, philosophic deduction, industry and literary power, the Reports of some of our younger civilians such as Messrs. Purser, Thorburn, Ibbotson, Wilson, O'Brien, and others.

out the hills over which they were chased like sheep by the Singh, and young men show where their fathers fought and fell. Destruction was so certain that the few villages which from the extreme difficulty of their position were either passed by the enemy, or, resisting attack, were but partially destroyed, claimed a triumph, and came to be looked upon as invincible.

'But the people of this unhappy district did not enjoy peace even during the respites which the withdrawal of the Sikhs afforded them; and it is hard to say whether they suffered most from these terrible but passing invasions, or from the bitter feuds which followed them, arising out of hostile acts committed towards each other, either to find favour with the invaders or to gratify personal feelings of hatred and revenge; for, as is common with people in such a depraved condition, they had no scruple in betraying each other for such purposes, and as spies or informers in bringing the Sikh scourge upon their neighbours with a baseness from which their ancestors would have revolted. One of the terms on which the Chamkain chief held his tenure of the Sikhs was the annual production of twenty Afrídí heads, and the old man relates without a blush the treacherous methods he was sometimes compelled to adopt to fulfil the conditions of his tenure.'

In the Settlement Reports of Colonel Cracroft and Mr. E. L. Brandreth of the Ráwal Pindi and Jehlam districts, we read:—

'Anarchy had reigned for centuries, and from the oldest times the district had been overrun by hordes of invaders, from Greeks to Afgháns. They swept through it and disappeared. The temporary desolation, the plundered homes, the deserted homesteads, were all things of the hour, and are now forgotten. But it was the rule of the Sikh Kárdárs, too far off from Lahore to be under any check, that reduced the Rájput and Ghakkar alike to their present state of poverty. Their rule was a military despotism, and their aim to exterminate all classes and families with any pretension to ruling power, and their strongest measures were accordingly levelled against the Ghakkars and all the gentry who shared with them in the management of the country. Accordingly we find them mere exiles or reduced to abject poverty, insomuch that they are now often compelled to become tenants under their former ploughmen. The high roads were universally unsafe. Passing through the limits of different tribes, travellers and caravans had to satisfy the rapacity of each by paying blackmail, or they had to submit to be plundered, outraged, and ill-treated, happy sometimes to escape with life.'

Regarding the Sikh rule in the central districts, Mr. Ibbetson writes:—

'In the centre and south-west of the province the Sikh rule was stronger and more equitable. In the earlier days, indeed, previous to and during the growth of the *misls*, it was nothing better than an organized system of massacre and pillage. But as the Sikhs grew into a people, and a national spirit developed, self-interest if nothing higher prompted a more moderate government. Still, as Sir Robert Egerton recorded, the Sikh population were soldiers almost to a man, and their one object was to wring from the Hindu and Muhammadan cultivators the utmost farthing that could be extorted without compelling them to abandon their fields. The Rájput especially, who had refused to join the ranks of an organization in which his high caste was disregarded, was the peculiar object of their hatred and oppression. Not to be for them was to be against them, and all who had any pretensions to wealth or influence were mercilessly crushed. They promoted and extended cultivation as far as was possible under a system which held forth the minimum of inducement to the cultivator, but they acknowledged nothing higher than the husbandman, they respected no rights and they recognized no property where such respect or such recognition conflicted with their pecuniary interests, and he who was not a Sikh, and therefore a soldier, was only valuable in so far as he could be utilized as a payer of revenue. Their rule was just and even in that they meted out oppression to all with an equal hand.'

Now let us see what Sikh rule was in the Rájput hills. The short-sighted Rájás had called in the Gúrkhas in their domestic squabbles, and, as with the frogs and King Stork, these fierce mountaineers established a reign of terror in the Kángra and Simla hills, till, after three years of anarchy, the fair Kángra valley became a desert, and the towns were depopulated. The Mahárájá Ranjít Singh and the Sikhs were called in, and the Gúrkha host departed like locusts. But the Sikh Kárdárs of the Mahárájá were not much better. Mr. Barnes, in his Settlement Report of the Kángra district, writes:—

'The Kárdár was a judicial as well as a fiscal officer. But his fiscal duties were most important. Corrupt judgments, or an insufficient police, were evils which might be overlooked even supposing they excited attention; but a Kárdár in arrears was an offender almost beyond the hope of pardon. The problem of his life was therefore to maintain cultivation at the highest possible level, and at the same time to keep the cultivator at the lowest point of depression. The burthen of the people was as heavy as they could bear; the utmost limits of toleration had been attained. A native collector is too discreet to ruin his tenants, but he will proceed to any lengths short of actual destruction. His policy is to leave nothing but a bare subsistence to the cultivator of the soil. But the assessment was generally equal, and the burthen, heavy indeed according to just and liberal principles, was still impartially distributed.'

Diwán Sáwan Mall, governor of Múltán, Leiah, Dera Ghází Khán, Khángarh, and Jhang, was the best of all the Mahárájá's administrators. Yet this is how Mr. O'Brien, who made the land settlement of Muzaffargarh, one of his districts, writes of him:—

'Diwán Sáwan Mall's government was better than anything that had preceded it. Its sole object was the accumulation of wealth for the Diwán. The execution of public works, the administration of justice and security of life and property were a secondary consideration, and were insisted on only because without them agriculture would not prosper, and the revenue would not be paid. When one examines his numerous cesses and sees how he levied dues to pay the people's alms and perform their religious duties, and then paid the poor and the Bráhmans what he thought a fair amount and pocketed the rest; how he levied a cess in return for keeping his word; and how he encouraged his officials to take bribes and then made them duly credit the amount in the public accounts, one's admiration for the great Diwán is less than it would be if based on written history [1].'

[1] I have no doubt that the description here given of the Diwán's procedure is correct, but I nevertheless believe that a much fairer general view of his administration is given in my biography of him and of Diwán Mulráj, his cruel and oppressive son, whose

Such extracts might be supplemented by a hundred others, recorded by British officers, whose task it has been, through the forty-two years since annexation, to efface the scars of the old wounds of the Punjab, and to bring back to the long-devastated province happiness, prosperity, and peace. But these will suffice to point the moral to those in India and in England who try to persuade the world that the British rule is harsh and oppressive, and who would make the greatest glory of our race, in the enlightened government of Hindustán, a matter for reproach and shame. Those who run may read, and the letters of light in which our Indian work is written can be seen by all eyes save of those who will not see. Anarchy, famine, and rapine have been replaced by orderly and just administration, under which every man enjoys his own in peace, none making him afraid. Where, out of twelve shillings' worth of produce, the Sikh Government took six from the peasant as rent, the British Government takes only two or one. The

treachery was a principal cause of the second Sikh War. The little peculiarities of administration recounted by Mr. O'Brien are venial in native eyes, and are common to almost every native administration, and I speak with experience, having been intimately associated with the administration of at least 100 native States in North and Central India. Diwán Sáwan Mall was on the whole a beneficent and wise governor, and though corrupt he was not oppressive. He turned what was a desert into a rich, cultivated plain. The people still revere his memory. His son Karm Náráin was also beloved, but Mulráj was hated. Popular sayings represent popular sentiment, and it was common to hear that Múltán was blessed with *sáwan* (the month of rain), Leiah with *karm* (kindness), while Jhang, the district of Mulráj, was desolated by *mula* (an insect that destroys the corn).

population has enormously increased, and the cultivated area in a still greater ratio. And if England were to withdraw her protecting hand, if she were to proclaim the *Pax Britannica* at an end and retire from India in a cowardly denial of her duties and her rights, is there any one of knowledge who doubts that in a very short time anarchy would return once more; that Sikhs, Maráthás, and Afghâns would again be fighting *à outrance;* that the children would again be tossed on the sword and spear-points of invaders, and the Punjab maidens again become the prey of the ravisher, while the light of flaming villages would nightly illumine the ancient walls of Delhi and Lahore?

CHAPTER VIII

HIS EARLY CONQUESTS

MAHÁRÁJÁ RANJÍT SINGH was the son of Sirdár Mahán Singh, the enterprising and unscrupulous leader of the Sukarchakia confederacy, and was born in the year 1780. His family was of the Ját Sánsi tribe, nearly related to the Sindhanwalias who were, at the time of Ranjít Singh's death, the most powerful of all the Sikh nobles north of the Beas, and who still take highest rank in the Punjab, although they now number no distinguished men in their ranks. The Sindhanwalias claim, like most other Sikhs, a Rájput descent, but they have also a close connection with the thievish and degraded tribe of Sánsis, after which their ancestral home, Rájá Sánsi, five miles from the city of Amritsar, is named.

The founder of the Sukarchakia and Sindhanwalia family was a bold and successful robber, Budha Singh, who, on his famous piebald mare Desi, was the terror of the country side. He was wounded some forty times by spear, matchlock or sword, and died at last in his bed, like an honest man, in the year

1718. His two sons, Chanda Singh and Nodh Singh, were as enterprising as their father. About the year 1730 they rebuilt the village of Sukarchak in the Amritsar district, and collecting round them a band of hard-riding Sikhs, seized several villages in its neighbourhood and in Gujránwála. From Chanda Singh the Sindhanwalia chiefs descended, while Nodh Singh was the direct ancestor of Ranjít Singh. He was killed at Majithiá, fighting the Afgháns, leaving one son, Charrat Singh, five years old, who became a powerful Sirdár, and took command of the Sukarchakia *misl*. Assisted by Sirdár Jassa Singh Ahluwalia, and the Bhangi confederacy, he repulsed Ubed Khán, the Afghán governor of Lahore, from his head-quarters, Gujránwála, with the loss of guns and baggage. He aided the Ahluwalia chief, Jassa Singh, who had been attacked and plundered by some of the Rámgarhias, to annex all their estates. He was killed by the bursting of his matchlock while engaged on an expedition against Rájá Ranjít Deo of Jammu, the cause of whose son, Brij Ráj Deo, he had espoused.

Mahán Singh, his eldest son, succeeded to the command of the confederacy, the influence and possessions of which he largely increased. But he was only eleven or twelve years of age when his father died, and a catastrophe seemed imminent. The Rájput Rájá had summoned to his assistance Sirdár Jhanda Singh, the head of the Bhangis; while the Kanheyas were aiding his rebellious son. The accident to Charrat Singh seemed likely to give the victory to the enemy, so his widow and Sirdár Jai Singh, the Kanheya leader, bribed a sweeper, who shot Jhanda Singh dead as he was riding with a few attendants through the camp. His death ended the quarrel, and the rival forces retired from Jammu.

In 1774, the year succeeding his father's death, Mahán Singh married Ráj Kour, the daughter of Rájá Gajpat Singh of Jínd, who, six years later, became the mother of Maháráját Ranjít Singh. It was significant that the marriage of this lady gave rise to instant discord, prophetic of the career of her son. Mahán Singh had come to Jínd with a great retinue and all the Phúlkian chiefs had assembled to meet him. During the festivities a dispute arose between the chiefs of Nábha and Jínd regarding a grass preserve belonging to the former, in which the Barátis or attendants on the bridegroom had been allowed to cut fodder for their horses. The agent of the Nábha chief attacked them, and a fight was the result, which so wounded the pride of the Jínd Rájá, the bride's father, that although he kept silence till the wedding was over, he determined on revenge, and soon afterwards, taking Hamír Singh of Nábha prisoner by stratagem, invaded his territory and seized a large portion of it, the estate of Sangrur being held to the present day.

For several years we hear nothing of the youthful Mahán Singh, but in 1780, when he may be assumed to have reached manhood, his famous son having been born, the Rájput prince of Jammu died, and Mahán

Singh commenced his career with a characteristic act of treachery. Rájá Brij Lál Deo succeeded his father and made friends with Mahán Singh, exchanging turbans as a sign of their lasting affection. Fortified by this alliance he thought that he might regain some of his lost estates from the Bhangi Sirdárs, and invited the Kanheyas, to whom he was tributary, to assist him. They at first assented but soon deserted him, and went over to the Bhangis, in alliance with whom they proposed to attack Jammu. The Rájá applied for assistance to his new brother-at-arms, Mahán Singh, who hurried northwards and attacked the Kanheya camp, but was repulsed with loss. Mahán Singh had to submit, and the Rájá was compelled to pay a tribute of Rs. 50,000 to Hakikat Singh, the Kanheya chief. Some months afterwards, this tribute falling into arrears, Hakikat Singh persuaded Mahán Singh to join him in a raid on Jammu, dividing the plunder between them. To this he assented, but marching by a different road and reaching Jammu the first, he found himself strong enough to attack alone, and, forgetting his sworn friendship to the Rájá as well as his agreement with the Kanheya Sirdár, he sacked and burnt the town and palace and retired with great spoil before the arrival of Hakikat Singh, who was naturally furious, but was unable to avenge himself, and died soon afterwards. The sack of Jammu brought upon Mahán Singh the wrath of the great Kanheya confederacy, and of its leader Jai Singh, who attacked him with such energy that he lost temporarily a large slice of territory, and had to sue for forgiveness. This was refused unless he gave up the plunder of Jammu, which the Sukarchakia chief was determined not to do. So he formed a coalition against the Kanheyas, among whom were Sirdár Jassa Singh Rámgarhia, who had been stripped of his estates some years before, and Rájá Sansar Chand, the Katoch Rájá of Kángra. The allies gave battle to the Kanheyas near Batála, their head-quarters, and defeated them with great loss. This was in 1784. Sirdár Jai Singh never recovered this defeat. He restored Kángra to the Katoch Rájá, and to Jassa Singh Rámgarhia all his lost possessions, and to Mahán Singh's son Ranjít Singh he gave in marriage Mahtab Kour, the infant daughter of his son Gurbuksh Singh, who had been slain in the Batála fight.

It would be tedious to relate the intrigues and violence with which Mahán Singh's brief career was filled. He was constantly at war with his neighbours and rivals, chiefly the Bhangis, although one of their most powerful leaders, Sáhib Singh, had married his sister. With this brother-in-law he was in frequent conflict for the two years preceding his death, as he wished to seize Sáhib Singh's town of Gujrát, about thirty miles north of his own capital of Gujránwála. It was while besieging Sáhib Singh in his fort of Sodhran that he fell seriously ill. Karam Singh Dula, a Bhangi chief of Chuniot, had hurried to the assistance of Sáhib Singh, and Mahán Singh at once attacked him; but, during the fight, he fainted away on his elephant, and the driver turned and carried his master from the field. The leader absent, the Sukarchakia troops fled, and the siege was raised; while Mahán Singh retired to Gujránwála, where he died three days afterwards, in the year 1792, when only twenty-seven years of age.

Although Ranjít Singh was only twelve years old when his father died, he had already accompanied him on expeditions. A Sikh in those days learned the art of war early. In 1790, his father was besieging Manchar, the fort of Ghulám Muhammad, chief of the powerful Mussulman tribe of Chattahs, with whom Mahán Singh was always fighting. Hashmat Khán, the uncle of the chief, climbed on the elephant on which Ranjít was sitting, and was in the act of killing the child, in which case the history of India and England would have been materially changed, when he was struck down by an attendant. When his father died the prospects of Ranjít Singh would have been very unfavourable had it not been for his mother-in-law, Sada Kour, who was not only a woman of the greatest ability, but had succeeded, as the widow and heiress of Sirdár Gurbuksh Singh, to the head of the Kanheya *misl*. This lady resolved, so far as she was able, to retain the power in her own hands, and use the force of both confederacies, Kanheyas and Sukarchakias, to break the power of all rivals. First she determined to be avenged on the Rámgarhias, who had joined in the attack on Batála, in which her husband was killed; and, in 1796, uniting her own troops with those of the young Ranjít Singh, she besieged Sirdár Jassa Singh Rámgarhia in his fort at Miáni on the Beas river. After defending himself for some time, his provisions fell short, and he asked for help from Sáhib Singh Bedi, the high priest at Amritsar. The Bedi sent a message ordering Sada Kour to raise the siege, but she, seeing her enemy was at last in her power, refused obedience. Again Jassa Singh sent an urgent message to the priest, who replied 'They will not mind me, but God Himself will aid you.' That very night the river Beas came down in flood, and swept away a large portion of the Kanheya camp, men, horses and camels. Sada Kour and Ranjít Singh escaped with difficulty, and retired to Gujránwála.

With this expedition the warlike instincts of the young chief seemed to awake, and he determined to become his own master and shake off the tutelage which had been imposed upon him by both mother and mother-in-law. The former was disposed of in a summary fashion. She was a dissolute woman, and chief among her lovers was Diwán Lakhpat Rái, who was the general manager of the estates during the minority. Ranjít Singh caused this man to be despatched on a dangerous expedition to Kaithal, where he was killed, and as some say with the connivance of Ranjít Singh. The lady disappeared; according to one report her son killed her with his own hands; according to another, he caused poison to be administered to her. But these stories are opposed to what we know of his character, which was singularly averse to deeds of violence except in fair fight; nor had he any respect for female virtue or fidelity. Mahtab Kour was probably shut up in a fortress, as an inconvenient intriguer, where she shortly afterwards died.

The yoke of the mother-in-law, Sada Kour, was far more difficult to shake off; and the young chief did not at first feel strong enough to attempt it. She had given the boy no education, and had encouraged him in all the sensual pleasures which are too often used by interested guardians in India to weaken the character and health of youthful princes whose power they desire to usurp or retain. Every day we see similar intrigues in the Feudatory States, with the same result. They severely test the tact and courage of the British Resident, and are sometimes treated too timorously by the Indian Foreign Office.

Ranjít Singh was fortunately possessed of an intellect which indulgence could not permanently cloud, and of a powerful physique which withstood for many years his habitual excesses. A special opportunity for distinction arose when Sháh Zemán, the grandson of India's frequent invader Ahmad Sháh, marched southwards to recover, if possible, his ancestor's lost provinces. In the year 1793 Zemán had succeeded Timúr on the throne, and two years later he invaded the Punjab, advancing no further south than the Jehlam river. But in 1797 and the following year he was more successful, and occupied Lahore without any serious opposition from the Sikhs, who pursued their usual tactics of avoiding a pitched battle, while harassing the rear-guard of the Afghán army and cutting off stragglers and plundering baggage. Some of the Sikh chiefs thought it would be well to keep on terms with Sháh Zemán, and paid homage to him at Lahore; Ranjít Singh, who had taken the opportunity of the Afghán invasion to raid the country south of the Sutlej, doing so by deputy, and when domestic troubles recalled Sháh Zemán to Afghánistán Ranjít returned to Lahore, which a happy chance allowed him to claim. Crossing the Jehlam in flood, the Afghán monarch lost twelve of his guns, and not being able to wait for their extrication, he promised Ranjít Singh, then master of that part of the country, the grant of the city and district of Lahore, with the title of Rájá, if he would send them to him. This task Ranjít Singh readily undertook and partly performed, rescuing eight guns and sending them to Pesháwar; and Zemán Sháh kept his promise. It was but a barren grant, and the Sikh chief was left to obtain possession as he best could.

The city of Lahore, which has existed for over two thousand years as a royal capital, had always been the object of desire to the Sikh Sirdárs, and during the eighteenth century had been won and lost several times. It was finally taken, in 1764, by Lehna Singh and Gujar Singh, two reckless Bhangi Sirdárs, who entered it through a drain one dark night, captured the deputy governor at a nautch, and were in full possession of the town by the morning. They divided the city into three shares, one falling to Sirdár Sobha Singh Kanheya, who was in the conspiracy, though he arrived too late for the surprise. When Ahmad Sháh made his last descent on the Punjab, three years later, he did not feel inclined to fight for Lahore, and confirmed Lehna Singh in its possession. The children of the partners were still in power when the grant was made to Ranjít Singh. But the sons of Lehna Singh and Sobha Singh were imbecile and debauched; and the third, Sáhib Singh, the only one of any ability, was absent. The people of Lahore disliked their extortionate rule, and Ranjít Singh was told that he would be welcomed as a deliverer. He accordingly marched with a strong force to Lahore, the gates of which were opened to him, and the two Sirdárs fled without offering any resistance.

The acquisition of Lahore in July, 1799, with the legally acquired title of Rájá, made Ranjít Singh, now in his twentieth year, a very powerful chief. The Sikh barons were filled with alarm at his success, and the Bhangis were especially anxious to avenge the capture of their principal town. In the following year a coalition was formed against him, the most prominent members of which were Sirdár Jassa Singh Rámgarhia, and Sáhib Singh and Guláb Singh Bhangis, and it was proposed to assassinate him during a conference to be held at Bhassin. But Ranjít Singh was too clever to fall into the trap. He took so large a force with him to Bhassin that the crime could not be attempted, and, after two months passed in hunting and feasting, he returned to Lahore. But he was aware of the designs against him on the part of the Bhangis, and resolved to anticipate them. In 1802 he sent to their head-quarters at Amritsar to demand the surrender of the famous Zamzama gun [1] which had been assigned to his grandfather Sirdár Charrat Singh as his share of the plunder when Lahore was captured in 1764. The Bhangis refused its surrender, on which Ranjít Singh attacked their fort at Amritsar, drove them to take refuge with the Rámgarhias, with whom they had divided the city of Amritsar, and annexed all their possessions.

By this bold and successful measure, Ranjít Singh became possessed of the two Sikh capitals, political and religious, and had little more to fear in his career of conquest, for the great Kanheya confederacy was already in his hand, and the famous Rámgarhia baron, Jassa Singh, was old and feeble, and Ranjít Singh knew that he had not long to wait before he should obtain his estates. He died the following year, and his eldest son and successor, Jodh Singh, who was a simple creature, though a brave soldier, became so devoted a follower of the Mahárájá (as we may now call Ranjít Singh) that it would have been superfluous villainy to have seized his territory. He swore eternal friendship with Ranjít

[1] This famous gun, of which a complete history is given at pp. 387-8 *Punjab Chiefs*, was cast at Lahore by Ahmad Sháh in 1761. It now stands in front of the Lahore Museum.

L 2

Singh, who flattered and cajoled him in every way, building his new fort of Govindgarh at Amritsar on the plan of the Rámgarhia fortress. He accompanied the Mahárájá on many of his expeditions. It was only on Jodh Singh's death, in 1816, when his successors began to quarrel, that Ranjít Singh marched against Amritsar, and after some severe fighting captured the fortress, which he razed to the ground, and then reduced the minor forts, about one hundred in number, and annexed all the vast territory of the confederacy in Amritsar, Jalandhar, and Gurdáspur. To the heads of the conquered family he assigned respectable jagírs, and gave them honourable appointments in command of troops or about his person.

The Nakkai confederacy was ruined in the year 1810. It will be remembered that Ranjít Singh had married a Nakkai girl, in 1802, who became the mother of his only child. But this alliance did not do the relations any good. When Káhn Singh, the nephew of Ráni Ráj Kour, became the head of the family in 1807, the Mahárájá tried to induce him to come and reside at court. But Káhn Singh knew that he should not be allowed to leave it again, *Vestigia nulla retrorsum*, and stoutly declined the honour. This did not save him, for the Mahárájá annexed all his estates, which were too close to Lahore, in Kasúr, Chúnian, and Gogaira, to be successfully defended. This incident is a fair example of the Mahárájá's methods. There was no pretended excuse, and Káhn

Singh, a near connection, had given no provocation further than that he was too weak to resist.

The last of the great confederacies to fall before the Mahárájá was the Kanheya, of which his mother-in-law, Mai Sada Kour, was the head. It has been already related that this lady had presented him with two boys, Sher Singh and Tara Singh, as the children of her daughter, Mahtab Kour. The fraud was, for reasons recorded in the next chapter, diplomatically accepted by the Mahárájá, who determined to repay it when an opportunity occurred. It came not till Sher Singh was about twelve years old, and had been sent in nominal command of troops to Hazára in the unfortunate expedition in which the gallant Diwán Rám Dyál had been killed at Gandgarh by the Yusafzais. On this occasion the young Sher Singh was said to have behaved well, and on his return the Mahárájá suggested to Mai Sada Kour, who had already adopted the boy as her heir, that the time had come when she might appropriately give up worldly affairs, and resign in favour of her grandson.

The old lady had no wish to perform this act of renunciation, but she was encamped at Sháhdera, a few miles from Lahore, and refusal might have unpleasant results. So she temporised, and returning to her head-quarters at Batála, opened negotiations with the English, asking to be permitted to come under their protection, and live in Cis-Sutlej territory. The Mahárájá heard of these overtures, and summoned the lady to his presence, where he repeated his orders with many threats. The same night Mai Sada Kour escaped in a covered litter; but was overtaken by troops, captured, and confined in a fortress, where she died soon afterwards, while the Mahárájá annexed all her great estates without any trouble: the only forts which held out being Atálgarh, which was gallantly defended by one of her women, and Mukeri, which gave Diwán Devichand, who had been sent to reduce it, a great deal of trouble. Batála was granted to Sher Singh in jagír, and the cunning lady who had manufactured this false prince fell into the pit which she had dug for others. At the same time it must not be forgotten that, with all her faults, Mai Sada Kour had acted well by the Mahárájá, who treated her with the blackest ingratitude. Her money and her troops had enabled him to seize Lahore and Amritsar, and had saved him from ruin in the doubtful years which followed his father's death.

CHAPTER IX

THE ENGLISH AND THE CIS-SUTLEJ TERRITORY

To one friendship the Mahárájá remained ever constant; from one alliance he never sought to shake himself free. This was the friendly alliance with the British Government, then represented in Hindustán by the East India Company. In the first years of the century, before he had appreciated the power and policy of the English, he was doubtful what line to adopt towards his new neighbours, and in December, 1808, had all but decided on war with them. But when his and their position was once defined and assured by the treaty of 1809, by which he renounced for ever all supremacy over the Cis-Sutlej chiefs, he frankly accepted the duties and responsibilities which the agreement imposed, and for thirty years remained the true and faithful ally of the British Government. He trusted its word with a calculated confidence which was astonishing in so suspicious and unscrupulous a ruler, and which, at the same time, was the highest proof of statesmanship. Nor was his confidence misplaced. The British Government invariably treated

Ranjít Singh in a spirit of frankness and friendship: they realized that he was a useful buffer between their unconsolidated provinces and the unknown, shadowy power beyond the passes of the North-West frontier, whence so many invading armies had poured down on the plains of Hindustán, and they never made a hostile movement against him. The Lahore State eventually fell from inherent weakness, and not from any designs on it by the British Government.

The story of the origin of the connection of our Government with the Cis-Sutlej States and the Mahárájá is a very instructive chapter of Indian history, but it is too lengthy to be told here in any detail. It is closely associated with the rise of the Maráthá power with its disciplined armies commanded by French generals, and with the romantic career of George Thomas, the English adventurer, who attempted, with much courage and audacity, to found a kingdom in Northern India, and came within a measurable distance of success. The mere outline of the situation is all that can be given [1].

The British power, at the beginning of this century, was spreading fast, like a rising tide, over Hindustán. The red line on the maps which marked its frontier was ever widening, and it was Ranjít Singh himself who truly prophesied that in time the whole of Hindustán would be red. Bengal, Benares, Oude, Allahábád, Cawnpore, Farukhábád, had in

[1] The history of these events is given in full detail in *The Rájás of the Punjab*, second edition, pp. 83–130.

turn fallen, when, on the 11th of September, 1803, General Lake defeated the Maráthá army commanded by Bourquien beneath the walls of Delhi; and, four days later, entered the capital of Hindustán as a conqueror. On the 1st of November the battle of Laswári was fought, when the Maráthás were again defeated with great loss; and Sindhia, by the treaty of Sirji Anjengaom, ceded Sirsá, Hissár, Rohtak, Delhi, Gurgáon, and Agra to the British Government. The three first-named districts were not, however, taken under British administration till the year 1809.

The Cis-Sutlej chiefs, who had made friends with the Maráthás, General Bourquien having just overthrown their enemy George Thomas, fought at Delhi against the English. They had miscalculated our strength, and during the whole of the year 1804 they gave great trouble in the neighbourhood of the Jumna, and ravaged the country up to the walls of Delhi. But after a severe defeat inflicted upon them by Colonel Burn on the 18th of December, 1804, they thought it prudent to retire across the river, and two of their most prominent leaders, Rájá Bhág Singh of Jínd, and Bhai Lál Singh of Kaithal, joined the English army, and afterwards remained fast friends.

In October, 1804, Jaswant Ráo Holkar, who had gained a great victory over Colonel Monson's brigade, besieged Delhi with a large force, but was repulsed by Colonel Ochterlony and Colonel Burn. Two months later, at Fatehgarh and Díg, the Maráthás were utterly routed by Generals Lake and Fraser, with great slaughter, while their leader Holkar, left without an army and after vain attempts to create one south of the Sutlej, went northwards to seek among the Sikh chieftains more trusty if not more efficient help than he could obtain from Sindhia, who hated him while he was compelled to appear his friend. Holkar remained at Patiála for some months, but its Mahárájá would not risk much to aid him, and the other Cis-Sutlej chiefs, seeing that his cause was hopeless, were equally discreet. At last, in October, 1805, Lord Lake having again taken the field against Holkar, he fled to Amritsar and endeavoured to obtain the alliance of Ranjít Singh, who was much inclined to assist him. But he was dissuaded from this step, which would have at once brought him into collision with the English, by his advisers Fateh Singh Ahluwalia and the Rájá of Jínd. Lord Lake pursued Holkar as far as the Beas, and had not the only thought of the Governor-General been to conclude a speedy peace, one of the most inveterate enemies the English have ever had in India would have been utterly destroyed. At this time the periodical fit of timidity had seized on the Court of Directors in London. They had been frightened at the bold policy of Lord Wellesley, the most eminent of all Governors-General, and the feeble Cornwallis had been despatched to reverse it.

Conciliation was foolishly considered to be wisdom. A treaty was made with Holkar which restored to him the greater part of the territory which had been wrested from him, and a supplementary agreement, dated the 1st of January, 1806, was made with Ranjít Singh and the Ahluwalia chief. This professed to be a treaty of friendship and amity between the Honourable East India Company and the Sirdárs Ranjít and Fateh Singh, by which the latter agreed to cause Jaswant Ráo Holkar to at once leave Amritsar and never again to hold connection with him, or aid him with troops, or assist him in any manner whatever. The British Government, on its part, promised that as long as those chiefs abstained from holding any friendly connection with its enemies, or from committing any act of hostility on their own part against it, the British armies would never enter their territories nor would the Government form any plans for the seizure or sequestration of their possessions or property.

These treaties, which excluded Holkar from the Punjab, practically secured Ranjít Singh from English interference in his plans of conquest north of the Sutlej. The country held by Sikh chiefs south of that river had not yet been the subject of arrangement, and in the summer of the same year 1806 the disputes of the Phúlkian Rájás induced Ranjít Singh to invade it. The condition of this unhappy country was melancholy in the extreme. The districts between the Sikh States and Delhi, acquired by the English in 1803, had been perhaps the most pitiable, but the lot of the peasantry in the Sikh portion of the tract was almost as bad. Mr. Denzil Ibbetson's Settlement Report on Karnál records:—

'So ended, in 1805, that terrible time called by the people the Sikh hurly-burly, or the Maráthá anarchy. Its horrors still live vividly in the memory of the villagers. The Sikhs never really established their grasp over the country south of Pánipat, and they held what they did possess only as feudatories of the Maráthás. But the whole period was a constant contest between the two powers, and the tract formed a sort of no-man's-land between their territories, and coveted by both and protected by neither, was practically the prey of the strongest and most audacious freebooter of the day. Even as early as 1760, Nádir Sháh had to approach Delhi by way of the Doáb, as owing to the constant passage to and fro of the Maráthá troops, the tract was so desolated that supplies were unprocurable, and forty years later, when we took over the district, it was estimated that more than four-fifths was overgrown by forest, and its inhabitants either removed or exterminated. The royal canal had long dried up, and thick forest had taken the place of cultivation and afforded shelter to thieves, vagabonds and beasts of prey. In 1827, Mr. Archer remarked that only a very few years had elapsed since this part of the country was inhabited wholly by wild beasts. Deserted sites all along the old main road still tell how even the strongest village had to abandon the spot where their fathers had lived for centuries and make to themselves new homes on sites less patent to the eyes of marauding bands. Revenue administration there was none; the cultivator followed the plough with a sword in his hand; the collector came at the head of a regiment, and if he fared well another soon followed him to pick up the crumbs.

It was at the invitation of his uncle Rájá Bhág

Singh, of Jínd, that Ranjít Singh, on the 26th of July, 1806, crossed the Sutlej with a large force, with the object of settling serious disputes which had arisen between that chief and the Mahárájá of Patiála. The English viewed his approach with some anxiety, and strengthened their garrison at Karnál; but he was too cautious to offend them, and contented himself with seizing the town and district of Ludhiána and Ghumgrána, which he divided among his friends. The Ludhiána family was of ancient descent, Muhammadan Rájputs, and it was represented by two widow ladies, whom Ranjít Singh plundered of all their possessions without remorse.

The next year, about the same time, he returned to Patiála with a large army under the command of Diwán Mokham Chand, and effected a settlement between the Rájá Sáhib Singh and his wife, the famous Ráni Aus Kour, much to the advantage of the latter, who had bribed him highest. On this occasion he seized on his return march many estates, Náráingarh, Wadni, Morinda, Zíra and others, chiefly in the Firozpur district, and distributed them among his adherents.

The Cis-Sutlej chiefs now perceived that by inviting Mahárájá Ranjít Singh to intervene in their disputes they had, like Frankenstein, created a monster whom they could in no way control. So in March, 1808, the Rájá of Jínd, the Bhai of Kaithal, Lál Singh, a very influential chief, with the agent of Rájá Sáhib Singh of Patiála, visited Delhi to ascertain from Mr. Seton, the Resident, if the British Government were prepared to extend to them their protection. This the British Government desired to do, but were uncertain how best to act. They wished to limit the ambition of the Mahárájá to the north of the Sutlej. But, at the same time, they were well aware of his determination to bring all Sikhs, south as well as north of that river, under his supremacy, and they were afraid of thwarting him so abruptly as to cause a rupture of friendly relations and throw him into the arms of France. For, however strange it may seem in these days, when the power of France in Hindustán is represented by two or three insignificant settlements, it was very different at the beginning of the century.

The Titanic contest between England and France, of which the prize was the commercial and colonial supremacy of the world, had been fought out in India as fiercely as elsewhere, and only terminated with the Peace of Versailles in 1783. Since then, the tradition of hostility and hatred of England had been fostered in native India by French generals of ability, like the Comte de Boigne, Perron and Bourquien, who turned the Maráthá hordes into a disciplined force in the same manner as Ventura, Allard and Court transformed, forty years later, the army of the Khálsa. After this, more terrible than the wrath of kings of France or the mad fury of the Republic, the shadow of the genius and ambition of Napoleon clouded the Asiatic as well as the European sky. The echo of the cannon of Marengo, Austerlitz and Jena reached

Teherán and Lahore, and there was no Asiatic Court which did not watch eagerly for news of the great conqueror who seemed to rival Alexander the Great or Tamerlane in the swiftness and sureness of his successes.

Nor was their anxiety uncalled for. The ambition of Napoleon knew no limits; and at one time he seriously proposed to revive the scheme of a French-Indian Empire, which might earlier have been founded by the illustrious Dupleix, had his ungrateful country supported instead of deserting him. In 1808, the time for realizing this dream had passed, and Napoleon's idea of establishing in Persia a secure base of operations and successively subduing Kábul and Lahore was beyond his strength. But the knowledge of his intentions disquieted the English Government, and it was to counteract them that Mr. Elphinstone was deputed to the Court of Kábul and Mr. C. T. Metcalfe to come to terms with Ranjít Singh.

The Mahárájá was quite astute enough to realize the embarrassments of the English, but was not in a position to profit by them. He felt himself anything but secure. The English were irritated by his invasion of Cis-Sutlej territory; the Afgháns were always ready to strike from the north; the Sikh barons of the Punjab proper were restive and suspicious; those whom he had subdued, eager for revenge; those whom he had not yet attacked, fearful of his treachery or violence. At the same time, his project of bringing all the Cis-Sutlej States under his rule and forming a kingdom which should include all the children of the Khálsa, was ever present with him, and he had reasonable hope of its accomplishment. His three Cis-Sutlej expeditions had shown him how weak were the Phúlkian Rájás and Málwá chiefs, so torn by petty feuds as to be incapable of uniting against him; while the English Government had, hitherto, made no direct remonstrance, and had even given the chiefs who sought its protection at Delhi an evasive answer. The announcement of the approach of the English envoy, who left Karnál in the middle of August, caused Ranjít some uneasiness, but he determined to strengthen his position before the negotiations should commence and formed an army at Kasúr preparatory to a new invasion of the Cis-Sutlej. Here Mr. Metcalfe arrived on the 11th of September, having visited Patiála *en route*, where the Rájá again begged for protection and vainly tried to induce him to take the keys of the city, to be restored to him on behalf of the British Government.

Mr. Metcalfe lost no time in placing before the Mahárájá the proposal which he was instructed to make of an alliance, offensive and defensive, against France, in the event of an invasion which both the Government and the Lahore State were equally interested in repelling. The Mahárájá cordially assented to the proposal, but required in return the acknowledgment of his sovereignty over all the Sikh States and people. This claim Mr. Metcalfe had no authority to concede, and as he held out little hope of a reference to Calcutta being successful, Ranjít Singh struck his camp and crossed the Sutlej, whither the Envoy, however displeased at the discourtesy shown him, had no option but to follow. From Khai to Farídkot, which was captured; from Farídkot to Maler Kotla, where a heavy tribute was demanded, Mr. Metcalfe accompanied the Mahárájá's camp, and it was only when the latter proposed to march to Ambála, in the very heart of the States seeking British protection, that the Envoy withdrew to Fatehábád. He had submitted a draft treaty to the Mahárájá which was only concerned with the alliance against France; while that which Ranjít Singh proposed in return asked not only for a firm alliance with England, but that no interference should be allowed in his disputes with Kábul, and that his sole and undisputed sovereignty over the whole Sikh country, north and south of the Sutlej, should be acknowledged.

The policy of the Mahárájá was skilful, bold, and deserved that success which it would probably have achieved had the danger of a French invasion been a real and not an imaginary one. He cared nothing for France, and felt that Napoleon was not his enemy but that of the English Government. If the English desired him to join them against France, they must be prepared to pay. So he pressed his claims on the Envoy and the Governor-General with insistence; he seized everything of Cis-Sutlej territory that he could while the negotiations were pending, in order that at their close, whatever the result, he might be left in possession of what he had actually conquered; and he cleverly kept the Envoy in his camp to weaken the resistance of the chiefs and to obtain some sort of official sanction for his enterprise.

After Mr. Metcalfe had left the camp, the Mahárájá continued his career of conquest; he seized Sháhábád and Ambála, and would have despoiled Patiála, but he knew that this would cause a breach with the English; so he contented himself with summoning the frightened Rájá Sáhib Singh to his camp, where he exchanged turbans with him and swore eternal friendship. He then returned to Amritsar, where he was rejoined by our Envoy on the 10th December.

Instructions had now been received from Calcutta. The impossibility of a French invasion was beginning to be realized, and a treaty with Ranjít Singh against so chimerical a danger was understood to be worthless, or, at any rate, not worth the concession of the authority of so strong and unscrupulous a ruler being extended over States which detested him and which had eagerly claimed British protection. The Mahárájá was accordingly informed that the Governor-General had learnt with great surprise and concern of his pretensions south of the Sutlej, and was still more astonished to find that he sought the assistance of the British Government in his designs. He was told that the Government was the successor of the Maráthás, whom they had defeated, and that during that contest the Mahárájá had himself suggested the Sutlej as a boundary. Since that time the Government had relieved the Cis-Sutlej chiefs from all tribute and would not allow them to be subjugated, but took them absolutely under its protection. It was further intimated that the Mahárájá's conduct to the Envoy had been discourteous and contrary to etiquette in invading Cis-Sutlej territory while a reference was being made to the Governor-General, and a demand was made that all territories seized south of the Sutlej since the first reference of the question to the British Government should be restored and the Sikh army withdrawn to the north of the river.

The Mahárájá vainly tried to evade compliance with these terms, of which he bitterly complained. The Envoy, he said, had been sent to conclude a treaty against France and cement a lasting friendship with him, but the treaty had been altogether forgotten, and the only friendship shown was in thwarting his most cherished policy. His disgust was such that he prepared for war. Troops and ammunition were collected from all quarters; the new fort of Govindgarh at Amritsar was armed and provisioned for a siege, and General Mokham Chand, the best of the Sikh generals and a bitter enemy of the English, was recalled from Kángra and marched to Phillaur on the Sutlej, opposite the town of Ludhiána, where he encamped. To this hostile movement the Government replied by sending a British force to Ludhiána under Colonel Ochterlony, who, passing Patiála and Nábha, was received with many demonstrations of satisfaction and regard. The negotiations at Lahore meanwhile progressed slowly. The Envoy was persuaded that the Mahárájá, who talked of joining his army on the Sutlej, had determined on war, and he advised the Commander-in-Chief to invade the Punjab as the best way of terminating a situation which was becoming intolerable. But wiser counsels at last prevailed with the Mahárájá, who saw that further resistance was hopeless, and on the 2nd April, 1809, he evacuated Farídkot and withdrew his Ambála garrison to the north of the Sutlej. No further difficulties were raised to the conclusion of the treaty, which was signed on the 25th April and ratified by the Governor-General on the 30th May following. By it the British Government agreed to abstain from any interference with the territories and subjects of the Mahárájá north of the Sutlej, while he agreed to respect the territories of the chiefs south of the river, who, in a supplementary proclamation, were assured of British protection, without interference in their rights and authority and without payment of tribute, subject to certain obligations of aid and assistance against any common enemy.

The history of the Cis-Sutlej States from this time until the first Sikh War was distinct from that of Lahore. The Mahárájá honourably observed his engagements, and, recognising that the power of the English was invincible, he frankly and for ever abandoned his dream of Cis-Sutlej supremacy and turned his attention to the expulsion of the Afgháns from the northern districts of the province, and the reduction of Múltán, Kashmír and the Deraját. Whether he was serious in preparing for war in the early part of 1809 is doubtful. Mr. Metcalfe certainly believed him to be so; but at that time the great sagacity and shrewdness of the Mahárájá were only imperfectly known, and it is more probable that he was only playing a game of brag to the last, in the hope that the British Government might withdraw a portion of their demands. In this he was partially successful, for he was only compelled to restore the Cis-Sutlej districts seized during his last campaign. Those of former years which he had retained or given to his Sirdárs were left to him, though he was not permitted to claim allegiance from the Cis-Sutlej chiefs even for lands which he himself had given them.

CHAPTER X

LATER CONQUESTS

A BRIEF sketch must now be given of the principal victories of the Mahárájá over Muhammadan rivals and enemies; the subjugation of the Mussulman tribes in the north and central districts, and the acquisition of Múltán, Kashmír, Peshâwar, and the Derajât[1].

The ancient city and district of Múltán were ruled by an Afghán family of the royal blood, who were appointed Nawábs in 1738, at the time of Nádir Sháh's invasion, when the Mughal Government was anxious to strengthen its outlying provinces by a system of decentralization which it was too weak to control. Between 1771 and 1779, the city was held, with some intervals, by the Bhangi Sirdárs, but they were finally ousted by King Timúr, and in the last-named year, Muzaffar Khán was appointed governor. He was a brave and energetic man, and held his own

[1] The full account of the Mahárájá's Múltán campaigns is to be found in the biographies of the Saddozni Chiefs of Múltán and Diwán Sáwan Mall, at pp. 475-489 and 272-285 of the *Punjab Chiefs*, and the Kashmír campaign in the biography of Diwán Mokham Chand, pp. 551-560

gallantly against both the Sikhs and the neighbouring tribes, Siáls and others, who attacked him. In 1802, Muzaffar Khán first saw the young chief Ranjít Singh, who had marched from Lahore to spy out the land. The Nawáb came out to meet him, thirty miles from the city, and the chiefs, having interchanged valuable presents, parted very good friends. Again, in 1806, after having reduced Jhang, Ranjít Singh marched towards Múltán and reached Mahtam, twenty miles north of the city, when the Nawáb, who had no wish to fight, gave him Rs. 70,000 to retire. The next year, his appetite whetted by what he had so easily won, the Maháráján returned and attacked Múltán in force. The town was in part captured, but the fort held out against all the Sikh efforts, and an agreement was concluded, through Sirdár Fateh Singh Kálianwala, by which the Maháráján retired on receiving a large sum of money. Nawáb Muzaffar Khán, weary of war, now made a pilgrimage to Mecca, and on his return vainly tried to induce the English to take him under their protection. But this the British Government declined. Múltán was remote and beyond the sphere they then desired to influence.

At the beginning of 1810, Ranjít Singh again marched against Múltán. He had just met the Afghán Sháh Shujá at Khusháb, and the exiled monarch wished the Sikhs to take Múltán and make it over to him. Muzaffar Khán had, in 1803, repulsed an attack of the Sháh's troops, and, in the hope of conciliating him, had more than once offered him an asylum at Múltán, but Sháh Shujá wished to obtain the city and province as his own by conquest. Ranjít Singh treated the weak-minded prince with great respect, but, failing to obtain any money from him, determined to take Múltán on his own account. On the 24th February, 1810, he arrived before the walls, and the next day took possession of the city.

For some time the fort was bombarded without effect; mining was then resorted to; but the besieged countermined with success, and blew up the battery of Attar Singh Dhári, killing him with twelve of his men. On the 21st of March a general assault was ordered, but the Sikhs were repulsed with great loss, and they now grew disheartened, for provisions had become very dear in the camp. Diwán Mokham Chand, the General, was dangerously ill, and several leaders had been slain, while scarcely any impression had been made on the citadel. On the 25th another assault was made with the same result. It was necessary to raise the siege, and Ranjít Singh, to his intense mortification, had to accept from Muzaffar Khán the terms which he had many times rejected, namely, two and a half lakhs of rupees, twenty war horses, and a contingent in time of war. Having received 30,000 in earnest of the ransom, the Mahárájá retired from Múltán on the 14th April.

Seeing that his own strength was insufficient for the capture of Múltán, Ranjít Singh addressed the Governor-General, requesting the co-operation of British troops. His proposition was not well received, the more so as he proposed that the force, instead of marching through the Punjab, should pass across the sterile country south of the Sutlej. Sháh Shujá even prepared for an independent attack on Múltán, but he was wise enough to relinquish an idea which could have had no chance of success.

In February, 1816, an irregular attack was made upon Múltán by the Sikhs. A strong force had been sent to Baháwalpur and Múltán to collect the tribute, and there being some delay in Muzaffar Khán's payment, Phúla Singh Akáli, mad and drunk with *bhang*, led a storming party of fanatics like himself against the town, and with such impetuosity did they make the attack that they gained possession of some of the outworks of the citadel. But Fakír Azizuddin made due apologies, the Nawáb paid his tribute quicker than he would otherwise have done, and the Sikh army proceeded towards Mankerá. In 1817 a Sikh army under Diwán Chand marched against Múltán and attacked the fort, but was repulsed, and retired on payment of ten thousand rupees. These attempts, however, were not made in earnest. The Maháráj was collecting his strength for a great effort, and had sworn that Múltán, which had so often defied him, should yet be his. During the cold weather of 1817 he was gathering supplies and men from all quarters, and in January, 1818, an army of 18,000 men, under the nominal leadership of Prince Kharak Singh, but in reality commanded by Misr Diwán Chand, marched from Lahore. On the way to Múltán, the forts of

Khángarh and Muzaffargarh were taken; the city was invested and captured early in February, and the bombardment of the fort commenced. The Nawáb had a garrison of only 2000 men, and the citadel was not provisioned for a siege, but he made a defence the like of which the Sikhs had never before seen.

Till the 2nd June the bombardment went on. Two large breaches had been made in the walls, for the great Bhangi gun, the Zamzama of Ahmad Sháh, had been brought from Lahore, and had been four times fired with effect. More than one assault was given by the Sikhs, but they were repulsed, on one occasion with the loss of 1800 men. The gates were blown in, but the garrison raised behind them mounds of earth on which they fought hand to hand with the Sikhs. The defenders of the fort were at length reduced to two or three hundred fighting men, most of them of the tribe or family of Muzaffar Khán. The rest had either been killed or had gone over to the enemy, for they had been heavily bribed to desert their master.

At length, on the 2nd June, an Akáli, by name Sádhu Singh, determined to surpass what Phúla Singh had done in 1816, rushed with a few desperate followers into an outwork of the fort, and, taking the Afgháns by surprise, captured it. The Sikh forces, seeing this success, advanced to the assault and mounted the breach at the Khizri Gate. Here the old Nawáb, with his eight sons and all that remained of his garrison, stood, sword in hand, resolved to fight to the death. So many fell beneath the keen Afghán swords that the Sikhs drew back and opened fire on the little party with their matchlocks. 'Come on like men,' shouted the Afghāns, 'and let us fall in fair fight.' But this was an invitation which the Sikhs did not care to accept. There died the white-bearded Muzaffar Khán, scorning to accept quarter, and five of his sons. A sixth was wounded severely in the face, and two accepted quarter and were saved. Few of the garrison escaped with their lives[1], and the whole city was given up to plunder. The fort of Shujábábád was also reduced and five guns taken from it. After this the walls of Múltán were repaired, a garrison of six hundred men was placed in the fort, and the Sikh army returned to Lahore. Múltán was known to be very wealthy, and the share of the Mahárájá amounting to only two lakhs of rupees he issued an order that all officers and soldiers should restore their plunder, and that if any was found with them after a certain date the penalty would be certain death. This order brought in some five lakhs to the State treasury, but the plunder of Multán was estimated at two millions sterling. It was supposed, in popular belief, to bring no luck to its possessors, most of whom died in poverty or were killed in battle[2].

In the spring of the following year, 1819, the Mahárájá annexed to his dominions the province of

[1] Mahárájá Ranjít Singh told the traveller Moorcroft that five hundred of the garrison survived and received quarter. This was incorrect. At the time of the last assault there were not 300 fighting men in the fort, and most of these fell at the breach.

[2] *Punjab Chiefs*, 487.

Kashmír, long coveted and many times vainly attacked, which more than doubled the area of his possessions. This strange and beautiful land of mountain and valley, rising in successive ranges from the low hills of Jammu and the Punjab border line to the giant peaks of everlasting snow double the height of the Alps, had been for several centuries the prize of successive conquerors, who specially valued it for its delightful climate in the summer months, when the plains of India were as a furnace, and the invaders from the north thought longingly of their cool and pleasant homes in Teherán and Kábul.

Until the beginning of the thirteenth century Kashmír had been ruled by its Hindu princes; then a Muhammadan dynasty succeeded for two hundred and fifty years; and, after several unsuccessful expeditions, Akbar the Great, in 1588, established the Mughal rule, which lasted for a century and a half. It was during this period that the fame of Kashmír for loveliness among the mountain regions of the world became so great. Powerful emperors, more wealthy and luxurious than any then reigning in Europe, Aurangzeb, Akbar, Jahángír and Sháh Jahán, made annual visits to its pleasant valleys, carrying with them their entire court, the transport of which exhausted the resources of the country. In Kashmír they built palaces and pleasure grounds, some of which still remain to testify to the magnificence and selfishness of the monarchs, who took so much from the people and gave so little in return.

The Mughal dynasty passed away, and was succeeded by the Afghâns under Ahmad Sháh Duráni, who conquered Kashmír in 1752, and ruled it, he and his successors, with a harshness and rapacity which made the Mughal yoke appear light. After seventy years, the Sikhs became the masters of the country, and they in turn gave way to the Rájputs. Rájá Guláb Singh of Jammu, the servant and counsellor of the great Ranjít Singh, was granted the sovereignty of Kashmír and its dependencies by the English in the year 1846.

It will be remembered that Jammu was closely connected with the fortunes of the Sukarchakia family, the father of the Mahárájá having plundered this city, then belonging to Rájá Brij Lál Deo, his unfortunate ally. Jammu, in those days, had no connection with Kashmír. It had been ruled for several thousand years by a Hindu dynasty of Rájput blood, and, although tributary to the Mughal Emperors, it had shaken itself free after their decline, and regained a short-lived independence, which was overwhelmed by the rising power of the Sikhs; first by the Bhangi Sirdárs, to whom Rájá Ranjít Deo was compelled to pay tribute, and then by the Sukarchakias under Mahán Singh. Ranjít Deo is still remembered in the hill country with genuine respect. He was a just judge and a liberal administrator, and it was a misfortune for his people that he was not strong enough to resist the wild Sikh levies, flushed with the new wine of religious enthusiasm, and as keen for the plunder of the orthodox Hindu as of the hated Mussulman. It was to this family that the three brothers, the Rájás Guláb Singh, Dhyán Singh, and Suchet Singh, the most powerful members of the Lahore Court, in the later days of the Mahárájá's life. belonged; or, at any rate, they produced a plausible genealogy which was sufficient to impose on the illiterate monarch and strengthen their claims to succeed to the Jammu heritage. Whether of princely descent or not, they certainly, in intelligence and personal advantages, were men of great distinction, and eminently deserved their success in a community where honest virtue was ridiculous and violence and fraud could alone ensure victory.

In the year 1811 the Mahárájá prepared for the conquest of Kashmír, and first reduced the hill States of Bhimbar and Rajáori, ruled by Muhammadan families of Rájput descent, and Kúlu in the following year. He then formed an alliance with Fateh Khán. Minister of Sháh Mahmúd of Kábul, who had crossed the Indus bent on the reduction of Kashmír and on the expulsion of the governor, Atta Muhammad Khán. The alliance was made only to be broken, both the Mahárájá and Fateh Khán determining to trick each other at the first opportunity; but it was necessary for the moment, as neither dared to march through the hills leaving a hostile army behind him. General Mokham Chand was placed in charge of the Sikh force, which was to receive a third part of the Kashmír plunder, and he marched with Fateh Khán from Jehlam. When, however, the latter had reached the Pír Panjál range, Fateh Khán, thinking that enough had been done to secure the Maháräjá's neutrality, pressed on by double marches with his hardy mountain troops, without giving Mokham Chand any notice of his intentions; while the Sikhs, never of much use in the hills, were unable to move owing to a heavy fall of snow. The Diwán saw the design of Fateh Khán, but he was not disconcerted. He promised the Rajáori chief a jagír of Rs. 25,000 if he would show him a pass by which he might reach the valley at the same time as Fateh Khán, which he contrived to do with a handful of troops under Jodh Singh Kalsia and Nihál Singh Attári. He was thus present at the capture of Shergarh and Hari Parbat and the reduction of the valley, which was a work of no difficulty, for the governor had fled and little resistance was offered; but his force was too small to be of much account, and Fateh Khán declared that the Sikhs were not entitled to their share of the spoil.

Sháh Shujá, the ex-king of Kábul, who had been detained a prisoner in Kashmír, was made over to Diwán Mokham Chand, and brought by him to Lahore, where the Maháräjá, much annoyed to hear that Wazír Fateh Khán refused to share the plunder, determined on revenge. He opened negotiations with Jahándád Khán, brother of the late governor of Kashmír, who held the fort of Attock commanding the passage of the Indus, and induced him to surrender it to a Sikh force. It was now Fateh

Khán's turn to be angry, and he demanded the restoration of the fort, but Ranjít Singh refused until he should receive his share of the Kashmír plunder. Fateh Khán, in April 1813, set out from Kashmír, leaving his brother, Azím Khán, behind as governor, and invested Attock. A relieving force was hurried up from Lahore, and Mokham Chand was again in chief command. For long the armies lay opposite each other, the Sikhs suffering somewhat in the frequent skirmishes and afraid to force a general engagement, till the garrison of the fort had exhausted its supplies, and it was necessary to relieve it or abandon it altogether. The Diwán then determined on fighting, and at Haidaru, a few miles from Attock, he drew up his force in order of battle.

It was opened by a brilliant cavalry charge led by Dost Muhammad Khán, afterwards the celebrated ruler of Kábul, which broke the Sikh line. One Sikh wing was thrown into complete disorder, and lost some guns. The Afgháns, thinking the victory won, dispersed to plunder, when the Diwán led up his reserves in person and drove back the enemy at all points with great loss. Fateh Khán had already fled, believing Dost Muhammad to be slain, and the Afghán army retired upon Kábul, whence the Wazír led an expedition against Herát to endeavour to recover the reputation he had lost before Attock. This action of Haidaru was fought on the 13th July, 1813, and was the first time that the Mahárájá had met the Afgháns in a pitched battle. It had important and far-reaching results. But the confidence which it gave to the Sikhs did not save them from a disastrous defeat the following year, when the Maháráján, believing that, with Fateh Khán absent and the Afgháns demoralised, he might seize Kashmír as an easy prey, massed an army at Siálkot on the plains below Jammu and prepared to march on the valley. Diwán Mokham Chand, the great general, was ill, and indeed died a few months later. He had strongly dissuaded the Maháráján from the undertaking, urging that the time was inopportune, the hill Rájás hostile, and the commissariat and transport insufficient. But the Maháráján would listen to no advice. He took charge of one division himself, and entrusted another to Diwán Rám Dyál, a gallant young man, a grandson of Mokham Chand, who had already won his spurs in several engagements. Rájá Agar Khán of Rajáori, where the army first halted, gave the Maháráján the advice to divide his force, one half under himself to proceed by way of Punch, and the other under Rám Dyál by the Bahramgalla route. The plan, which may have been necessary from the difficulties of transport on hill roads, had the unfortunate result that the one division could not render any assistance to the other, and that an active enemy could destroy both in detail. This was done by the governor of Kashmír. He attacked Rám Dyál with his whole force as the Sikhs, thoroughly exhausted by a fatiguing march, descended from the Pír Panjál pass into the valley. Rám Dyál fought well, but was overpowered by numbers, and lost a large number of men. He contrived, however, to fight his way to a strong position in the valley, and waited for reinforcements, which the Mahárájá sent him under Bhaya Rám Singh, an unenterprising officer, who failed to relieve him, and returned to the Mahárájá. Ranjít, finding that an advance was impracticable in presence of the superior and victorious force of the enemy, determined to retreat. The hill Rájás rose behind him; heavy rain turned the streams into torrents and made the road impassable, and it was only after great difficulty and heavy loss that Ranjít Singh fought his way out of the hills and reached Lahore. Rám Dyál, left to his own resources, behaved so gallantly that Azím Khán was compelled to come to terms with the enemy he could not annihilate, and gave him a safe conduct to the Punjab.

This was a disastrous expedition, and the Mahárájá's generalship was much at fault. But his perseverance was more remarkable than his strategical ability, and the next year he was on the watch for another opportunity to seize Kashmír. This did not at once arrive, for Wazír Fateh Khán returned from Herát and Kábul and joined his brother Azím, the governor, and the two united were too strong to attack. Ranjít Singh was, however, able to avenge himself on the Rajáori Rájá for his treachery, and burnt his palace and town. The opportunity came in 1819, when the Mahárájá, taking advantage of the absence of the governor, sent a strong force into Kashmír under the command of

Misr Diwán Chand, who had the year before taken Múltán, while Rám Dyál commanded the rear division. This last was prevented from marching by heavy rain, and had no share in the fighting. But little resistance was made. Zabar Khán, the *locum tenens*, took to flight, and the province of Kashmír was annexed by Ranjít Singh to his dominions; Moti Rám, the son of Diwán Mokham Chand and father of Rám Dyál, being the first governor.

The history of the province from this time until its grant by the English to Rájá Guláb Singh differs little from that of other Sikh districts except that, being far removed from Lahore, the governors were able to fleece the people with more than the usual impunity. Sometimes the oppression they exercised was so intolerable that insurrection, the popular reply to official tyranny, warned the Mahárájá that it was time to replace an obnoxious lieutenant by one less rapacious. The Diwáns Moti Rám and his youngest son Kirpa Rám were, on the whole, the best governors that the valley had in these hard days, and their rule, with two breaks, lasted till 1831. The former was an indolent man who did not trouble himself much about administration, but he was kind-hearted and liked by the people. When his eldest son Rám Dyál was killed in Hazára in 1820, he resigned the appointment and wished to retire to Benares, and the Mahárájá sent as his successor the fighting Sirdár Harí Singh Nalwa. But his ideas of government were so primitive that the Kashmírís revolted, and it was necessary to send back Diwán Moti Rám, who remained in charge till 1826, when the family fell into disgrace owing to the sinister influence of Rájá Dhyán Singh, and Diwán Chúni Lál, a man of no account, took his place for a year and a half. Then Diwán Kirpa Rám became governor. He was intelligent, with unusual ideas of magnificence for a man of the trader class, and beautified the capital with many fine buildings and pleasure grounds. The Rámbágh garden at Srínagar, where stands Maháráj́á Guláb Singh's monument, was laid out by him.

In 1828 Kashmír suffered much from earthquakes; many public and private buildings were destroyed, with great loss of life. After the earthquake came the cholera, a worse epidemic than that which had ravaged the province in the time of Moti Rám. In 1831, Kirpa Rám again incurred the enmity of Rájá Dhyán Singh. He had given protection to Rájá Faiz Talab Khán of Bhimbar, whom both the Dogra Rájás hated and wished to capture; while Kirpa Rám resolutely refused to give him up. He was recalled from Kashmír, and soon afterwards left the Punjab for Benares, to join his father. His family for three generations had done good and brilliant service for the Maháráj́á, but this did not save them from the ingratitude of their master, who cared nothing for men whose work was done, or who had become obnoxious to a new favourite. This absolute selfishness of Ranjít Singh, and the shameful manner in which he ignored faithful service were the most unpleasing features in his character. Diwán Mokham Chand, the founder of the Diwán family, was his best and most successful general, and it was in great measure owing to his military ability that the Mahárájá established himself as sole ruler of the Punjab. But this did not save his son Moti Rám or his grandson Kirpa Rám from constant slights, fines, confiscation and eventual ruin.

The conquest of Kángra with the surrounding hill districts had been completed by the Mahárájá in 1809, and was signalised by one of his usual acts of treachery. Rájá Sansar Chand Katoch was the head of the noblest Rájput house, and was generally respected for his abilities as much as for his ancient family. During the last quarter of the eighteenth century, when everything was in confusion, he extended his rule over all the neighbouring Rájput States, and successfully withstood many combinations made against him. In 1784, he obtained from Sirdár Jai Singh Kanheya the famous Kángra fort, a place impregnable by the arms and artillery of those times, and the possession of which gave the control of the neighbouring country. The Mahárájá had long determined to oust him from this point of vantage, and the opportunity came when the Gúrkhas, on the invitation of the Kehlor Rájá, Mahán Singh, invaded Kángra and invested the fortress. The siege was protracted for years and Sansar Chand might at last have wearied out his persistent enemy, had he not, in an evil hour, asked for the assistance of Ranjít Singh, who intrigued with both sides and gained possession of the fortress by pretending to be a relief sent by the Nipalese general, Amar Singh Thappa. Once inside, he laughed at both Rájputs and Gúrkhas, and held it for himself. The ruse was brilliant and worthy of such admiration as history gives to successful treachery.

It was not till many years afterwards that the Mahárájá Ranjít annexed the whole of the Kángra States and added it to his own dominions. The great Rájá Sansar Chand had died, and his son, Anrodh Chand, was the tributary chief in his room, when Rájá Dhyán Singh, the Mahárájá's evil genius, ever anxious to justify his claim to pose as the legitimate representative of the ancient house of Jammu, persuaded his master to demand the hand of one of Anrodh Chand's sisters for his son, Hira Singh, a handsome boy who had become a great favourite at court. The proud Rájput, who, from the heights of his Katoch ancestry, looked down upon the Dogra Rájás as upstarts, refused the alliance, and fled from Lahore with his family across the Sutlej to British protection. The Mahárájá, furious at the rebuff, forthwith confiscated all his estates, and the following year, 1829, desiring to humiliate the Rájput prince, he himself married two of the illegitimate half-sisters of Anrodh Chand, one of whom died before Ranjít Singh, and the other became *Satí* at his death.

The conquest by the Mahárájá of Peshávar and the hill country of Hazára, which was a difficult and lengthy operation, costing him much in money, officers, and troops, must be briefly noticed, together with the reduction of the Muhammadan tribes of the Punjab, who were quite as fond of fighting and as gallant soldiers as the Sikhs themselves. What they did not possess was the power of organization and combination, for which the Mahárájá was so conspicuous, and which enabled him to subdue separately tribes which united might have successfully resisted him. There was no Mussulman of genius to gather together his co-religionists under the green flag of the Prophet, and to found, in the Northern Punjab, a Muhammadan kingdom to rival and counterbalance the Sikh monarchy of Lahore. A few fanatics like Syad Ahmad Sháh, at the head of heterogeneous assemblies of mountain warriors, gave at times an infinity of trouble, and preached a holy war against Sikhs and infidels; but their fierce enthusiasm burned out as quickly as straw, and they could only destroy and not build up. The victory rested, as it was bound to rest, with the slow-witted, strong and stubborn Sikhs, directed by the persistence of their great Mahárájá, slow, and sure, and irresistible as the rising tide.

This sketch of the Sikhs and their master would give to English readers a very false idea of the Punjab if it allowed them to conceive it as a province chiefly inhabited by a Hindu population among which the unorthodox sect founded by Govind Singh rose to sudden and exceptional importance. The Punjab is to-day, and was in Ranjít Singh's time, almost equally divided between Hindus and Muhammadans. In the large towns of the south and central districts there is a considerable Mussulman element, but, generally, it may be said that the districts east of the Chenáb river are Hindu, and those to the west are Muhammadan. As we approach the North-West frontier and the mountain ranges, the percentage of Hindu residents continually diminishes, until, in the frontier districts, the population is almost entirely Muhammadan, the exceptions being the traders and money-lenders who are almost always Hindus, and who flourish even in the fanatical cities of Central Asia. Many of the Muhammadan tribes are of great importance and antiquity, and special mention may be made of the Ghakkars, Jodrahs, Janjoahs, Awáns, Tiwánas, Siáls, Kharrals, Khattars, Ghebas and Kokhars who inhabit the plain country west of Lahore, or the broken and hilly regions between the Indus and the Chenáb rivers[1]. Some few of these claim a foreign descent; the Ghakkars from Persia; the Awáns from Afghánistán or from the Bactrian Greeks; but it is doubtful whether this signifies more than may be affirmed of all the Aryan races of India who were the product of successive waves of foreign conquest. Little is to be found in the records of these tribes to show that their antecedents differ in any important particular from the Rájputs or the Játs. They are, in as true and complete a sense, children of

[1] The detailed history of these tribes is given in the *Punjab Chiefs*, pp. 502 to 606.

the soil, autochthones, as any of the Hindu tribes, and their early adherence to the creed of Islám has rather served to stereotype their racial peculiarities than to change or impair them. The close connection between many of these tribes is well known. The Tiwánas, Siáls, Ghebas and the Daudpútras of Baháwalpur have all descended from a common ancestor, although the latter amuse themselves by tracing back their lineage to Abbás, the uncle of the Prophet Muhammad. But these, with most of the ancient tribes of the Punjab, are of Rájput descent. It seems probable that three important Rájput invasions occurred in the Punjab. The first was antecedent to all historical records, perhaps not later than 2500 years B.C., and the princes of Katoch and Chamba and the Jálandhar hills, whose ancestors ruled over the Bári and Rechna Doábs, are its living representatives. The second immigration was a thousand years later, when Ujamida, the son of the founder of Hastinapur, led his Yádu Rájputs to the north of the Jehlam and founded a dynasty which ruled the country from Ráwal Pindi to Múltán. Lastly came the emigrations from the south, extending over a long series of years, from the tenth to the fifteenth centuries of the Christian era, when Rájputs of many and various races came to the Punjab, the descendants of whom are the Játs, Tiwánas, Siáls, Ghebas, Kokhars and many well-known tribes.

The Punjábi Muhammadans form a very important part of the native army of India. Although I have said that the Sikhs, taking them all round, in peace and in war, in the demoralising quiet of cantonment life or in the fierce delights of a campaign, are the finest military material in India, yet the Punjábi Muhammadan is not far behind. In battle his wild enthusiasm is perhaps more irresistible, and his bravery and love of fighting are equally great. But his steadiness in the face of inaction, reverse, or defeat is not equal to that of the Sikh, nor is he so content to serve on garrison duty, in peaceful times, far from his native land. He is not so universally useful as the Sikh; so unemotional, so ready to take the good and the evil of military service with an equal mind. But he is a splendid fighter, and the Tiwánas, Siáls, and Múltánis gained much distinction both in 1849 and 1857 fighting on the side of the English.

The Mahárájá first attacked and subdued those tribes which were in the near neighbourhood of Lahore. First came the Kharrals, who held some 40 villages about Shaikhopura and Jhang, a turbulent and thievish race, ever impatient of control. More fanatical than other Muhammadan tribes, they submitted with the greatest reluctance to Hindu rule, and it was as much as Diwán Sáwan Mall and the Sikhs could do to restrain them, for whenever an organized force was sent against them they retreated into the marshes and thick jungles, where it was impossible to follow them. The Mahárájá annexed their country in 1803, and then turned to their neighbours, the Siáls, who inhabited the tract about

Jhang, Leiah and Chuniot. He exacted a ransom of Rs. 60,000 a year from Ahmad Khán, the chief, and three years later seized the country, farming it to Sirdár Fateh Singh Kálianwala. The Tiwánas were too strong to be openly attacked at this time, though, in this same campaign of 1803, the Mahárájá treacherously entrapped Khán Beg Khán, one of the tribal chiefs, and made him over to his brother, who put him to death, Ranjít Singh taking a lakh of rupees as the price of blood. It was not till 1817 that he seriously attacked the Tiwána chief at Núrpur and took the fort; and though Ahmad Yár Khán, the then chief, regained his territory, it was only for a short time, and with the aid of the Nawáb of Mankerá, a rival and enemy, he was compelled to make final submission to Ranjít Singh. An opportunity for revenge on Nawáb Háfiz Ahmad Khán of Mankerá soon arrived, when the Mahárájá attacked him in 1821. The Tiwánas joined in this expedition with enthusiasm. It was a difficult work, for Mankerá was situated in the true desert, and was surrounded by a cordon of twelve forts, within which no wells had been sunk. But the perseverance of the Mahárájá, who commanded in person, overcame all the physical difficulties of the undertaking. He moved steadily on, sinking wells as he advanced, and at last invested the fort, which, after a siege of twenty-five days, surrendered; the Nawáb being allowed to retain the governorship of Dera Ismáil Khán, a most troublesome district, which the Sikhs were unable to control.

The Tiwánas had shown so much gallantry during this campaign that the Mahárájá took fifty of them to Lahore as his personal body-guard. They are certainly a most picturesque race, and I well remember the rival Tiwána chiefs, Fateh Sher Khán and Sher Muhammad Khán, at the great Vice-regal Darbár of Lord Lawrence in 1864, at Lahore, as the most splendidly handsome of all the nobles in that historic gathering. The town of Kasúr, about fifty miles south of Lahore, was the head-quarters of a powerful Muhammadan family of Pathán origin, who had successfully held their own against the Sikhs during the latter half of the eighteenth century, and who had joined the cabal against Ranjít Singh when he obtained possession of Lahore in 1800. The Mahárájá attacked them several times, and, in 1807, he marched with all his forces against Kasúr, and drove out Nawáb Kutbuddin, who retired to his estate of Mamdot on the south bank of the Sutlej which is still held by his descendants.

The chivalrous tribe of Ghakkars, who played a conspicuous part in Indian history, and ruled Kashmír for many years, and had fought, not without glory, with invading emperors, was never able to make much head against the Sikhs after the signal defeat of Sultán Mukarab Khán, in 1765, by Sirdár Gujar Singh Bhangi under the walls of Gujrát, which then, with a large part of the Ráwal Pindi, Jehlam and Gujrát districts, was a Ghakkar possession. They were crushed by the exactions of the Mahárájá's deputies, Budh Singh Sindhanwalia and Raja Guláb Singh of Jammu, and, in 1818, their last semblance of authority was swept away. It was reserved for the English Government to restore, in some degree, the fortunes of this ancient race.

The Awáns were a tribe too scattered to make an effective resistance to the Sikhs. Their principal village, Shámsábád, was destroyed by General Mokham Chand in 1813, to punish them for their involuntary hospitality to the Kábul army while investing Attock. But their hereditary holdings in Ráwal Pindi, Jehlam, and Sháhpur were not interfered with, though they had to pay tribute to the Sikh governors of the district. The same remark applies to the Janjoahs, who had a friendly partnership with Mahán Singh, the father of the Maháráját.

The Chibs, an ancient Rájput tribe, scattered through the low hills bordering the Kángra, Jammu, and Gujrát districts, had, in great part, become Muhammadan, although, in Kángra, they retained their original faith. They had been often attacked by the Bhangi Sirdárs and also by Sirdár Mahán Singh Sukarchakia, but their country was difficult and their reduction was left to the Maháráját himself. After taking Gujrát from Sirdár Sáhib Singh, in 1810, Ranjít Singh marched against Chúnian and Mangha, the two strong forts of Rájá Umr Khán, the Chib chief, who was compelled to submit, and on his death, a few months later, the whole of his possessions were confiscated.

The same year the Maháráján marched against Fateh Khán, the Baluch chief of Sáhiwál, a man of great influence, who had successfully withstood the Bhangi Sirdárs, and had won back from them many conquered districts. The father of the Maháráján compelled him to pay a small tribute, which, in 1804, Ranjít Singh largely increased. But it was paid with some irregularity; an excuse for annexation, which the Maháráján readily availed himself of. In 1810, he marched against Fateh Khán and captured his fort by surprise, carrying him to Lahore, where he was given a sufficient jagír and lived for a few years, till tired of a life of inaction he fled from court, and, hunted from one asylum to another, died at Baháwalpur, in exile, in 1820.

Thus all the Mussulman chiefs and nobles fell, one by one, under the supremacy of Maháráján Ranjít Singh, and by the year 1820 his power may be said to have been consolidated and absolute throughout the whole Punjab proper, from the Sutlej to the Indus. To the south it was opposed by the British Protectorate, and in the north by the Afghán rulers of Kábul, who claimed, by right of conquest and in the name of Ahmad Sháh Duráni and Timúr, the sovereignty of Northern India.

The battle of Haidaru has already been noticed, in which the Sikh army defeated Wazír Fateh Khán and Dost Muhammad Khán, afterwards Amír, under the walls of Attock. Then followed the repulse of Diwán Rám Dyál in Kashmír, with the disastrous retreat of the Mahárájá, and the final subjugation of the province in 1819. The work of subduing the fierce Mussulman tribes of Hazára, who have so often given trouble since the English conquest and have necessitated numerous military expeditions, was a very difficult matter. The Sikhs were never fond of hill fighting, while the Afgháns and Yusafzais are much more at home in the hills than in the plain country, and their national system of attack has been developed by the wild and mountainous nature of the country in which they fight. The governor of Hazára, Sirdár Hukma Singh Chimni, who had been, in 1814, appointed to the command of Attock and Hazára, after he had by a brilliant feat of arms driven the Afgháns out of the Attock fortress (which they had recovered by a *coup de main*), was a brave soldier, but a ruthless administrator. His arbitrary ways and especially his hanging of a wealthy and influential chief, Syad Khán, had roused the whole country side, and compelled the Mahárájá to recall him in 1819, and appoint Diwán Rám Dyál in his place.

This young and incautious general, accompanied by Prince Sher Singh, as nominal commander, and Sirdár Fateh Singh Ahluwalia, marched through the hills as far as the fort of Gandgarh, where the tribes of Yusafzai and Swát had assembled to oppose them. The Sikhs were outnumbered, and the tribes had gained confidence by more than one victory over the troops of the late governor. The fight was kept up the whole day till sunset, when the Sikhs, tired out, returned to their entrenchments. Diwán Rám Dyál, with a small personal escort, was among the last to leave the field, and the enemy, seeing him separated from the main body, attacked him with impetuosity, and after an obstinate resistance killed him and all his followers. When the Sikhs saw that their general was dead they were much disturbed, and the next day retreated, burning all the villages in their track. The loss of Diwán Rám Dyál was much felt by the army; but there were many good officers to take his place, chief of whom were Sirdárs Hari Singh Nalwa and Budh Singh Sindhanwalia, the Maháréjá's cousin. He was succeeded in the governorship of Hazára by one of the Majíthia Sirdárs, Ámar Singh, who was not more fortunate than Rám Dyál, and was killed by the Dhúnd and Tarin tribes in precisely the same manner, being surprised with his escort while resting after a sharp engagement.

The city and province of Pesháwar became tributary to the Maháréjá in 1823. It was then held for the Afghán monarch by Yár Muhammad Khán, whose brother, Muhammad Azím Khán, had succeeded Fateh Khán as the nominal minister but virtual ruler of Kábul and Northern Afghánistán. The latter, displeased with his brother, the governor of Peshávar, for making terms of friendly and subordinate alliance with the Maháréjá, marched with a strong force from Kábul, and, raising the wild Yusafzai tribes in a *jihád* against the Sikhs, met them in battle at

Theri, near Naoshera, halfway between Attock and Pesháwar. It was a critical contest, and decided, once for all, whether Sikhs or Afgháns should rule east of the Kháibar and the mountains of the North-West frontier. The Mahárájá commanded in person on the left bank of the Kábul river, where the Yusafzais were posted. The Akális the Sikh fanatics, and the Gházis the devotees of Islám, met in fair fight, which resulted in the repulse of the former with the loss of their much-feared leader, Phúla Singh. But the Mahárájá repulsed the tribesmen; while, on the other side of the river, Sirdár Harí Singh Nalwa, commanding the main body of the Sikh army, with General Ventura, Jamadár Khushhál Singh, and Sirdár Budh Singh Sindhanwalia, opposed the Afgháns under Muhammad Azím Khán, who did not make much of a stand, but retired upon Pesháwar and thence through the passes, while the Mahárájá occupied and plundered the city. He then retired, leaving Yár Muhammad Khán as governor, subject to payment of an annual tribute.

From this time onwards, Hazára, Pesháwar and the frontier districts were a constant source of trouble and expense to the Mahárájá, and in frequent conflicts with the Bárakzái chiefs and the untamable and fanatical tribes he lost many of his best officers and troops. The long and monotonous record of frontier fights can find no place in this brief sketch. The situation was aggravated by the appearance of a religious leader, Syad Ahmad Sháh, a Muhammadan of Nasírábád, in the North-Western Provinces, who with the righteous purpose of defending his creed and co-religionists against Sikh attack, emigrated to the Peshâwar hill country and preached a *jihád* or holy war against the infidels. This man was the founder of the sect of Indian Wahábís, who have at different times given much trouble to the Indian Government, though many of them are a loyal, law-abiding people, distinguished from other Muhammadans by a simpler and purer worship. Others, a fierce, fanatical and seditious body, have always been in opposition to the Government, and in times of trouble have tried to stir up hatred and disaffection. But while a *jihád* against the British Government, which gives more absolute religious liberty to Muhammadans than is enjoyed in any Mussulman country, has usually been recognised by Indian Muhammadans as illegal, a *jihád* against the Sikhs, in 1823, was a very different matter. During the time of their supremacy the Muhammadans had persecuted the Sikhs and killed their prophets and defiled their temples, and now the day of vengeance had come and the men of Islám were rolled in the dust by the triumphant followers of Govind Singh.

Sirdár Harí Singh Nalwa had been appointed governor of Hazára, and his harsh conduct and hatred of Muhammadans was always causing fanatical outbreaks. In 1824, there was an insurrection in Drá-band (*Darband*), and the following year he was nearly overwhelmed by a gathering of the Yusafzais, five times as numerous as the Sikh force, whom he defeated after a most stubborn and gallant fight. To his assistance Sirdár Budh Singh Sindhanwalia, a splendid soldier, was despatched. This cousin of the Mahárájá had become suspect, and Ranjit Singh sent him to the frontier in the hope that the chances of frontier service would prevent his return to Court. The origin of his disgrace was this. In 1825, the Mahárájá was ill at the Rámbágh, in Amritsar, and his physicians had given him up. Budh Singh, one of the most powerful chiefs, with his reckless brothers Attar Singh and Lehna Singh, determined to be prepared for the worst, and attempted to surprise the fort of Govindgarh at night, rightly thinking that the possession of this fortress would give an immense advantage to its holder in the scramble for territory and power which would follow the death of the Mahárájá. He heavily bribed the officers in charge, and forged an order in the Mahárájá's name for the surrender to him of the fortress; but the commandant, Jamadár Khushhál Singh, suspected treachery, and declared that he would not open the fort gates at night to the Mahárájá himself. So the plot failed; and the Mahárájá recovering and hearing the story, a change of air to Hazára was considered advisable for Budh Singh. Here he did excellent service. At Akora he fought Syad Ahmad Sháh and defeated him, but lost five hundred men. The next day he advanced to Jagíra, where he was joined by the Dogra chiefs and the Attári Sirdárs, the whole force amounting to 10,000 men with twelve guns. Their entrenchments were soon surrounded by the large but undisciplined army of the Syad, composed of Kábulis, Yusafzais and Afgháns. For some days the Sikhs remained in their entrenchments, exposed to the incessant assaults of the enemy, till, at length, the supplies and patience of Budh Singh being exhausted, he led his men against the enemy, and after a severe fight defeated them with great slaughter. The Syad took refuge in the Yusafzai hills, and it was two years before he recovered his strength sufficiently to again take the field.

The Mahárájá and Harí Singh Nalwa had both advanced to the relief of Budh Singh, but, finding their assistance was not needed, they marched to Pesháwar to punish the Afghán governor for the encouragement which he had uniformly given the Syad. The city was pillaged, the palace of the Bála Hissár burnt, the mosque defiled, and many of the trees, for which the Pesháwar valley is famous, were cut down. The tribute was increased, and the Mahárájá carried away with him as a hostage the son of governor Yár Muhammad Khán.

Continual fighting, raids and insurrections marked the Sikh connection with Pesháwar and the frontier till 1833, when Sháh Shujá, whose real power was nominal, but who still maintained the style of kingship, ceded to Ranjít Singh, Múltán, the Deraját and Pesháwar. But the gift had to be taken by fraud or force, and Prince Nao Nihál Singh and Sirdár Harí

Singh were sent with 8000 men, under pretence of demanding enhanced tribute, to seize the city. By a ruse, pretending a wish to inspect the walls, the Prince obtained possession; the Bárakzái Sirdárs fled, after brief resistance, and the Sikhs occupied the coveted position. But the Afgháns were not disposed to allow them to hold it without opposition. In 1835, Amír Dost Muhammad Khán invaded the district with the intention of retaking the city; but Fakír Azizuddin, who was sent ahead of the army to delay his advance, was so successful in his mission that the Sikhs arrived in great force, and so nearly surrounded the Afgháns that the Amír had hastily to retreat beyond the passes.

The reduction of the frontier was a matter beyond the Sikh strength. After the capture of Pesháwar, Prince Nao Nihál Singh made a military promenade in force through the districts, burning, plundering, and collecting what revenue he could, and Diwán Hákim Rai, the most prominent of rebels in 1849, was appointed governor of Bannu, Tank, Dera Ismáil Khán, and Isákhel; but the Sikhs never obtained any real control of this wild strip of country, and their influence ceased beyond the range of their forts. They never collected revenue except by armed force, and every two or three years marched an army through the districts to sweep up their arrears. This was amusingly shown when, in 1847, after the war, the attention of Colonel Lawrence, the British Resident, was called by Rájá Dina

Náth, the Chancellor, to the outstanding revenues of Tank. 'There are nearly two years' revenue unpaid,' said the Rájá, 'so it is about time to send an army.'

Sirdár Harí Singh Nalwa remained at Peshávar as Commander-in-Chief, and, in 1836, was ordered to build a fort at Jamrúd to command the entrance of the Kháibar Pass. This work was soon finished, of no great strength, but sufficient to overawe the Afrídís and annoy any force marching from Kábul. The Amír was furious, and determined to take up the challenge thus thrown before his mountain gateway.

He despatched a force of 7000 horse, 2000 matchlock men, and 18 guns from Jalálábád under his son Muhammad Akbar Khán, three other of his sons accompanying, and being joined by some 20,000 tribesmen, they arrived in April, 1837, before Jamrúd, then unprovisioned and garrisoned by only 800 Sikhs. Harí Singh was ill with fever in Peshávar and made no sign, and the siege went merrily on for six days, when the walls were breached so that cavalry might have charged up them. At last, when hope was almost gone, the great general turned out all his garrison from Peshávar, 6000 foot, 1000 regular cavalry, and 3000 irregular, and marched to the relief.

For some days the hostile forces lay opposite each other, neither wishing to attack. At length Harí Singh decided on battle. His advance was, at first, irresistible, and the Afghâns broke and fled; but the Sikhs carried their pursuit too far, and were overwhelmed by a charge of Afghán horse under Sirdár Shamsuddin Khán. Harí Singh, seeing a desperate effort could alone retrieve the fortunes of the day, rode with his principal Sirdárs to the front and by his presence and example encouraged the Sikhs to stand. The day might still have been won, but Harí Singh fell, mortally wounded by two bullets in the side and stomach, and his men, disheartened fell back under the walls of Jamrúd and waited for reinforcements. These at last arrived, when the water and provisions had been exhausted, and nothing remained for the besieged but to cut their way through the enemy as best they might. But when the news of the Afghán attack first reached Lahore, a large part of the force which had been assembled to do honour to the marriage of Prince Nao Nihál Singh, was despatched north in all haste. The Prince himself, his father Kharak Singh, General Ventura, Jamadár Khushhál Singh, and all the flower of the Sikh chivalry, formed so formidable an array that, on their timely arrival at Peshâwar, the Barakzái Sirdárs raised the siege and withdrew without further fighting to Jalálábád.

During these years of storm and stress the Mahárájá had maintained a strict alliance with the British Government, which was now, on its own account, inspired by evil counsels, to commence a course of interference in Afghánistán with the intention of setting aside the bold and capable family that had seized power, in favour of the most feeble and incapable of all the effete Saddozái race. The negotiations with Lahore, the arrangements with Ranjít Singh and Sháh Shujá, the successful commencement of the enterprise and the overwhelming catastrophe of its close, have all been told in detail elsewhere. Here there is no space to dwell upon them. The campaign was eminently distasteful to the Mahárájá, who recognised that it was undertaken with the intention of circumscribing his power in the directions of Sind and Afghánistán, as formerly it had been limited on the Sutlej. But, so far as he was able, he furthered the plans of the Government as explained to him by Sir William Macnaghten in May, 1838, and prepared to bear his share of the burthen of the campaign if only he was permitted by his chiefs, with whom any co-operation with the English was specially obnoxious. For the personal influence of the Mahárájá was waning, and the Jammu Rájás Dhyán Singh and Guláb Singh were all-powerful at Lahore.

In the cold weather of 1838, when the British army destined for the Afghán campaign was concentrated at Firozpur, and the Governor-General, Lord Auckland, was visiting the Mahárájá in great state at Lahore, a second stroke of paralysis, caused by excesses, anxiety and excitement, warned Ranjít Singh that the time had come when he must leave the scene of his conquests for ever. From this time till his death the following year he was only half alive, yet he still endeavoured to conduct business, and sometimes he was mournfully carried in his palanquin at a parade of his troops on the plain below the Samman Burj of Lahore. But all knew that the end must soon come, and each of the powerful Sirdárs whom the fear of their master had alone restrained from flying at each other's throats, prepared for the struggle which was inevitable on his decease.

On various occasions he had been attended by English doctors, Murray in 1826 and M'Gregor after his paralytic seizure in 1834, but he had not found their prescriptions of much avail, partly from the intractable nature of the disease, partly because he would not give up hard drinking. He also tried electricity and galvanism. The visit of the Commander-in-Chief, Sir Henry Fane, with a number of English officers on the occasion of the marriage festivities of Prince Nao Nihál Singh, in March, 1837, had done the Mahárájá no good; for he thought it due to hospitality to set an example of drinking, which prepared him for the second paralytic stroke in 1838. During his last illness, Fakír Azizuddin, who was his medical adviser as well as his secretary, attended him with the utmost devotion, administering the medicine with his own hand and telling him news from all quarters. Other famous native practitioners were summoned; but he refused to see the English doctor whom the Governor-General sent him. But medicine could not cure him, even if the musk, ambergris, pounded pearls, sandal and almonds, which formed an important part of the native pharmacopœia, did not hasten the end. He summoned to his bedside Prince Kharak Singh, his only son, and proclaimed him his heir, with Dhyán Singh as minister, a triumph which that wily fox was not destined to enjoy for long. Then, after having given twenty-five lakhs of rupees in alms to the poor and to the priests of Nánkhána, where the first Guru was born, and to those of Dera Bábá Nának, where he died, the great Mahárájá was moved, according to Sikh and Hindu custom, from his bed to a carpet on the ground, where he breathed his last on the 27th June, 1839.

The six years which followed were a period of storm and anarchy, in which assassination was the rule and the weak were ruthlessly trampled under foot. The legitimate line, Kharak Singh, the imbecile, and his handsome, reckless, vicious son, Nao Nihál Singh, was soon extinguished in blood. Then came the turn of the impostors: Mahárájá Sher Singh, a drunken debauchee, murdered together with his son by the fierce Sindhanwalias; and Dhulíp Singh, the son of the dancing girl, whose end would have been as swift and bloody as the others had not a propitious fortune and the collapse of the Sikh army allowed him a secure refuge in the unrequited generosity of the British Government.

As Ranjít Singh had sown, so was the harvest. The fathers had eaten sour grapes and the children's teeth were set on edge. The kingdom founded in violence, treachery and blood did not long survive its founder. Created by the military and administrative genius of one man, it crumbled into powder when the spirit which gave it life was withdrawn; and the inheritance of the Khálsa passed into the hands of the English, who will hold it against all comers if only they rule with the justice, beneficence and strength which alone make empires enduring.

INDEX

THE END.